RATIONALITY, POLITICS AND HUMAN RIGHTS

Includes schematic diagrams charts

Adriano Sousa Costa
Henrique Hoffmann M. de Castro

Preface Dra. Flávia Piovesan

ABOUT THE AUTHORS

Adriano Sousa Costa

Member of Academia Goiana de Direito.
PhD in Political Science by UnB (Brazil).
MSc in Political Science by UFG.
Columnist of Conjur.
Professor at Escola Superior da Polícia Civil de Goiás.
Professor of post-graduation at CERS, MeuCurso and Verbo Jurídico.
Columnist by Conjur.
Goiás Civil Police Commissioner
e-mail: professoradrianoscosta@gmail.com

Henrique Hoffmann Monteiro de Castro

Professor and principal of post-graduation at Verbo Jurídico.
Columnist of Conjur and Rádio Justiça from STF.
Professor at Escola da Magistratura do Paraná and Escola Superior de Polícia Civil do Paraná.
Was a professor at CERS, TV Justiça from STF, Secretaria Nacional de Segurança Pública, Secretaria Nacional de Justiça, Escola da Magistratura Mato Grosso, Escola do Ministério Público do Paraná, Ciclo, Curso Ênfase, CPIuris and Supremo.
MSc in Law by UENP.
Bachelor of Law by UFMG (Brazil).
Paraná Civil Police Commissioner.
www.henriquehoffmann.com

CONTENTS

Title Page

About the Authors

Copyright

Foreword

Preface

Chapter 1. Inter-American Human Rights System and Commission — 1

Chapter 2. Theory of rational decision — 13

Chapter 3. Costs of implementing IACHR solutions — 38

Chapter 4. Factors influencing the IACHR's solutions' implementation — 54

Chapter 5. Human rights implementation: compliance with IACHR cases — 60

Chapter 6. System correction measures — 127

Chapter 7. Conclusion — 131

Notes — 138

References — 149

FOREWORD

Since its first uses, human rights denote different interpretations. Understanding them as moral rights, as ideas and arguments that lead human actions and political institutions, moved landmarks and historical documents. The liberal tradition affirms them both in the pages of thinkers like John Locke and Jean-Jacques Rousseau and in moments like the French Revolution and the USA's Declaration of Independence. If, on the one hand, human rights as moral rights have in universality their conviction strength, after all everyone who shares the human condition would be its holders, on the other hand, its materiality would be fragile, since its protection would not materialize within the courts and other spaces for implementing standards.

However, human rights can also be understood as legal rights, as part of a public normative body of law. The (also) liberal tradition that claims them stress the construction of the so-called 'Rule of Law' out of the right-duty dyad, calling on the state entity to both protect such rights and to be limited by them. Human rights as legal rights may even appeal to universality, but such employment has moral nature's argumentative rhetoric characteristics, and in order to justify its quality as 'juridical' it needs to be 'positivized' through legitimate processes and institutions. Human rights thus make sense in a court or in an operator's legal piece.

This human rights differentiation as moral rights or as legal rights is necessary for the philosopher Jürgen Habermas. In Faktizität und Geltung, or Law and democracy: between factuality and validity in the English translation, Habermas deals with the crucial law relevance in modern societies, especially in the constitutional democratic state. Although human rights have what Habermas called the 'face of Janus' and are geared to both law and morality, the faces' separation imposes itself for the German philosopher. Human rights, for Habermas, support universal validity, as moral norms, but gain facticity because they structurally belong to a coercive and positive legal order. If law is "the modern normative law, which presents itself with the intention of systematic reasoning, mandatory interpretation and imposition",[1] human rights are rights in the legal sense in the Habermasian conception. Its legitimacy occurs from the processes of legal positivization (Rechtssetzungsprozesses), observing the democratic public sphere's necessary procedures and institutions.

Habermas' text deals with human rights in connection with popular sovereignty, in order to affirm the co-originality between human rights and democracy. His central concern is more with the 'domestic' processes of this correlation, although in later texts Habermas himself has turned to international bodies, especially the European Union.

Like Habermas, many thinkers and operators are dedicated to making human rights operational. Affirming them in addition to moral rights as legal rights, without losing their moral value, is an urgent task in a scenario where only their declaration is insufficient for their uses. Although we cannot lose sight of the theoretical debates and controversial interpretations involving human rights, studies that are dedicated to understanding them in their employment are becoming increasingly urgent in contexts of increasing oppression.

This work is a daring and necessary study. It treats human rights as a legal right, as part of a legal process of producing legal obligations. It goes beyond the current studies on the Inter-American Commission and its relations with States: it wants to analyze how the result of what the international institution produces is understood by those that it intends to affect behavior, the States. Its conceptual approach is daring in so far as it is inspired by the theoretical model of rational choice, as well as in a tool for public policies to analyze the solutions of the Inter-American Commission on Human Rights.

The authors offer the public a work that combines methodological rigor, empirical ambition and analytical skills. The research results are thought-provoking and counter intuitive, which increases its relevance for those who want to better understand international institutions, public policies and human rights. The fields of law, political science and international relations benefit greatly from this contribution.

João Roriz

Professor of International Relations, College of Social Sciences, Federal University of Goiás. PhD, University of Oxford. PhD, College of Law, University of São Paulo.

PREFACE

It was with great joy that I accepted the special invitation to preface this work.

The Inter-American Commission is responsible for protecting and promoting human rights in the Americas. Under Article 41 of the American Convention on Human Rights, the Commission has the primary function of promoting the observance and defense of human rights and, in the exercise of its mandate, has the following functions and duties: a) to stimulate human rights' awareness in the peoples of America; b) make recommendations to the Member States' governments, when deemed appropriate, to take progressive measures in favor of human rights within the scope of their domestic laws and constitutional precepts, as well as appropriate provisions to promote due respect for those rights; c) prepare studies or reports that it considers convenient for the performance of its duties; d) request the Member States' governments to provide it with information on the measures they take in the human rights area; e) To attend the consultations that, through the General Secretariat of the Organization of American States, formulate the member states on issues related to human rights and, within their possibilities, provide them with the advice that they request; f) act with respect to petitions and other communications, in the exercise of its authority, in accordance with this Convention's articles 44 to 51 provisions; and g) submit an annual report to the General Assembly of the Organization of American States.

Promoting, monitoring and protecting human rights in the region are the Inter-American Commission's main vocation, in combining conciliatory (for example, in seeking to reach friendly solutions between States and victims, when rights are violated); adviser (for example, when recommending the measures adoption measures for States to promote human rights);

criticism (for example, when reporting on the human rights situation in an OAS member State, after being aware of the State's arguments, when these violations persist); prosecutor (for example, when preparing studies on human rights issues, in order to promote their respect); protective (for example, when acting in cases of extreme gravity and urgency, in order to avoid irreparable damage to people); and preventive functions (for example, by stimulating the human rights culture in the region, through technical cooperation, with training programs for the most diverse social actors, strengthening institutionality and public policies with a focus on human rights, considering regional diversity).

The Inter-American Commission has played an extraordinary role in the regional protective parameters dissemination related to the human dignity safeguarding (the so-called "inter-American corpus iuris"), which symbolize a minimum protective floor and not a maximum protection ceiling. Such protective parameters have provided compensation for national deficits, promoting advances in legislative frameworks and public policies in the field of human rights, as well as preventing setbacks in the rights protection regime.

The transforming inter-American system's mandate is based on three essential components: the absolute victims' centrality (the inter-American system's raison d'être, which justifies and legitimizes their very existence); the inter-American corpus juris (as a regional civilizing heritage encompassing inter-American standards); and the institute of integral reparation (structural violations have structural causes, which demand the inter-American system's transformative impact through guarantees of non-repetition capable of promoting structural changes in public policies and regulatory scope).

In this context, the exquisite study is included, which I am honored to preface. It is a consistent, solid and innovative research, which takes as an empirical universe of analysis the recommendations and agreements contained in the IACHR follow-up report published in 2017, assessing its compliance degree, with emphasis on the costs of implementing public policies by the States. The main focus of the work is on the State and the economic, institutional, legal and political costs of complying with inter-American recommendations.

Relevant hypotheses are tested during the analysis, including: a) whether solutions from less complex cases are more likely to be complied with; b) if the form of the demand solution (whether friendly or meritorious) influences the propensity to comply; c) whether federated or unitary States have a greater or lesser compliance degree with the solutions; and d) whether States and societies considered freer are more likely to comply with decisions.

One of this exquisite study's important conclusions is the greater probability for friendly solutions to be fully complied with, when compared to solutions called meritorious. The Inter-American Commission itself, in its extensive institutional experience, confirms this hypothesis that the participation of those involved in the process of building the solution increases its full compliance probabilities. In accordance with the Strategic Plan of the Inter-American Commission, the goal of expanding the friendly solutions use stands out.

It was also concluded that in the free regimes the compliance possibilities are increased, since they do not have the institutional and ideological resistance of less free regimes. Federated models impose even greater complexity and difficulty for the full compliance with decisions, than non-federated models, according to research findings.

With high methodological rigor, the study's greatest ambition is to identify factors capable of increasing states' compliance with inter-American recommendations, considering the government's rationality, based on an overall tool effectiveness rate.

Strengthen the inter-American system's effectiveness and enhance its impact, assessing its driving factors, as well as different orders' governmental costs (institutional, economic, political and legal), thus appear as the central objective of this book.

The Inter-American System has saved and saves lives. It allowed for dictatorial regimes' destabilization; demanded justice in democratic transitions; and now demands the improvement of democratic institutions by combating human rights violations and protecting the most vulnerable groups.

In ensuring the safeguarding of rights, the Inter-American Commission has played an important role in consolidating minimum protective parameters in defense of human dignity, promoting internal advances in relation to legislative frameworks and public policies in the region.

The present work offers a qualified and valuable contribution to strengthening the inter-American system's effectiveness and its transformational impact in the region.

Flávia Piovesan

PhD in Constitutional Law and Human Rights at PUC-SP; visiting fellow of the Human Rights Program at Harvard Law School (1995 and 2000); visiting fellow at the Centre for Brazilian Studies at the University of Oxford (2005); visiting fellow from the Max Planck Institute for Comparative Public Law and International Law (Heidelberg - 2007; 2008; 2015-2019); Humboldt Foundation Georg Forster Research Fellow at Max Planck Institute (Heidelberg - 2009-2014); Visiting Scholar of the David Rockefeller Center for Latin American Studies, Harvard University (2018); she was a member of the UN High Level Task force for the implementatiton of the right to development and a member of the OAS Working Group to monitor the San Salvador Protocol on economic, social and cultural rights. Member of the Inter-American Commission on Human Rights (2018 to 2021).

CHAPTER 1. INTER-AMERICAN HUMAN RIGHTS SYSTEM AND COMMISSION

1.1. Inter-American Human Rights System

After the Second World War, discussions arose about the need to establish an international network for the protection of human rights, given the failure of States to fulfill this mission. Totalitarianism broke with the human rights paradigm, denying the value of the human person, in a true objectification of the human being. In this context, if there had been an effective system of international human rights protection before the war, perhaps barbarism could have been avoided.[2] Because of this atrocious period in history, humanity came to understand the supreme value of human dignity, in around which several fundamental rights gravitate, as well as the need for immediate implementation of a global model to safeguard the rights of all.

No matter how much the countries internally establish control and protection bodies in order to protect human rights (with support especially in the constitutions of each country), when this defense fails, the need for safeguarding made by international bodies created for this purpose comes up. This was one of the formulas found worldwide to prevent acts of inhumanity, similar to those experienced in that period of armed conflict, from happening again.

The organization of political society must be done in a way that not only legitimizes power, but also establishes a brake on it,[3] making the common good possible through both actions and abstentions. And if that control does not work at the national level, society must be able to create international mechanisms to deal with violations of people's rights. In this sense, the State's inability to resolve a dispute at the national level may lead to its solution at the international level.

In this scenario, international treaties and conventions were published in a movement for the internationalization of human rights. It is in this panorama that international systems for the protection of human rights are inserted, through a Global System based on organs (United Nations) and international treaties (mainly UN Charter and Universal Declaration of Human Rights), in addition to regional systems also organ-based (Organization of American States) and international conventions (especially OAS Charter, American Declaration of Human Rights and Duties and American Convention on Human Rights).

Regional protection systems have more advantages when compared to the global system, given the existence of a certain cultural, political and economic homogeneity in countries, thus facilitating standardization in dealing with issues related to human rights.

This humanistic approach is also facilitated by the fact that there are intense commercial connections between these countries. The fear of disruption in economic relations can strengthen this type of system, as international discredit in the humanistic context has the strength to affect business and political relations between the violating country and the other members of the bloc.

Although there were initial questions against the establishment of regional human rights systems, especially on the part of the United Nations (with its emphasis on universality), the benefits of having such systems are now widely accepted. Countries in a given region often have shared interests, including protecting human rights in that part of the world, with the advantage of proximity as a reciprocal behavioral influence factor, facilitating agreement on common action standards, something that the global system does not offers.[4]

The Inter-American Human Rights System formally began with the approval of the 1948 American Declaration of Human Rights and Duties, as well as the OAS Charter, which establishes the fundamental rights of the human person as one of the founding principles of the Organization.

Despite the importance of the Inter-American Human Rights System, membership of the countries that make up the Organization of American States (OAS) is optional. This is not an obstacle for the Inter-American Commission on Human Rights to act also in the face of countries that have not adhered to the inter-American regional system, unlike what happens with the Inter-American Court (which needs the country's express adherence to legitimize this action).

> Article 44. Any person or group of persons, or a non-governmental entity legally recognized in one or more member states of the Organization, may submit petitions to the Commission containing complaints of violation of this Convention by a State Party. (...) Article 61. 1 Only States Parties and the Commission are entitled to submit a case to the Court's decision. (American Convention on Human Rights)

The Commission, created in 1959, has a privileged position in the inter-American system. It is the Inter-American Commission on Human Rights (IACHR) that receives thousands of petitions[5], only a portion of which are referred to the Inter-American Court of Human Rights. In summary, the Court only receives demands that are not resolved within the Commission.

It should be noted that, since the American Declaration of the Rights and Duties of Man was not a mandatory instrument, containing prescriptions of a moral nature, there was no adequate curbing of violations of fundamental rights, which is why the OAS realized the need for a mandatory protection document. In this context, the American Convention on Human Rights was approved. The ACHR established the inter-American human rights system based on two main institutions: the Commission (already in operation) and the Inter-American Court of Human Rights. In effect, the Inter-American Human Rights System started to present two distinct aspects: one developed from the OAS Charter (which involves all OAS member states), and the other based on the Convention (mandatory only for the signatory countries of the document).

Double strand of the Inter-American Human Rights System	
OAS Charter	American Convention on Human Rights
all member States	signatory countries of the document

The Commission is competent to act on the basis of the OAS Charter, the ACHR and also the Statute of the IACHR and the Rules of Procedure of the IACHR, having jurisdiction over all OAS member states, which makes it the central organ of the system. This is because the other base body, the Inter-American Court, has restrictions of action in some countries that do not recognize their jurisdiction or are simply not signatories to the Convention.[6]

Base organs of the Inter-American Human Rights System	
Inter-American Commission on Human Rights	Inter-American Commission on Human Rights
central organ	
jurisdiction over all OAS member States	performance restricted to signatories to the Convention who recognize their jurisdiction

This dual role of the Commission in the Inter-American System is a unique characteristic of this hemisphere, giving it different features from the European system.[7]

1.2 Inter-American Commission on Human Rights

The OAS, an organization that brings together the independent countries of the Americas, is based on four fundamental pillars: democracy, human rights, security and development.

The Commission is a main and autonomous body of the OAS. The IACHR is made up of seven independent members, specialists in human rights, who do not represent any country and are elected by the OAS General Assembly. The Commission has technical and administrative support from the executive secretariat.

The Inter-American Commission on Human Rights is competent to examine violations of human rights protected by various inter-American human rights treaties.

Inter-American Human Rights Treaties	
American Convention on Human Rights	Inter-American Convention to Prevent and Punish Torture
Additional Protocol to the American Convention on Human Rights in the Area of Economic, Social and Cultural Rights	Protocol to the American Convention on Human Rights Regarding the Abolition of the Death Penalty
Inter-American Convention to Prevent, Punish and Eradicate Violence Against Women	Inter-American Convention on Forced Disappearance of Persons
Inter-American Convention on the Elimination of All Forms of Discrimination against Persons with Disabilities	

In addition to acting in individual cases, the IACHR prepares country reports, addressing systematic violations or violations related to structural problems in a given state. However, when depositing the Convention, Brazil made a reservation that the Commission can only carry out on-site visits and inspections with the express consent of the Brazilian State.

Pillars of the work of the Inter-American Commission on Human Rights		
Individual Petition System	monitoring the human rights situation in Member States	attention to priority thematic lines

A violation of human rights, as long as it is not resolved internally, can be filed by petition for analysis by the IACHR. This is an elementary condition to legitimize the performance of the Commission, considering that the absence of an internal solution to the case is what brings out antagonistic interests between the violating State and the victim (or legal representative). The exhaustion of domestic remedies is a way of allowing the State to resolve disputes within its own legal system, since - for the dualistic view's defenders - international law was conceived as a subsidiary system to domestic law.

This complementarity of the IACHR to the action of the State can be seen expressly in the text of the American Convention on Human Rights (ACHR), with other requirements stipulated in Article 46.

Admissibility requirements for a petition or communication by the IACHR
that domestic remedies have been filed and exhausted, in accordance with the generally recognized principles of international law
that is presented within a period of six months, from the date on which the presumed harmed in his rights has been notified of the final decision
that the subject of the petition or communication is not pending in another international settlement process
that, in the case of Article 44, the petition contains the name, nationality, profession, domicile and signature of the person or persons or the legal representative of the entity submitting the petition.

The internal judicial remedies that must be exhausted are those that are adequate and effective. A judicial remedy is appropriate when its filing is able to protect the violated right. For example, habeas corpus in the event of a forced disappearance. On the other hand, a judicial remedy is effective when it can obtain the result for which it was created. For example, the court decision rendered without undue delay.

However, exceptionally, the Commission may study a request in which domestic remedies have not been exhausted.

Exceptions to the exhaustion of domestic remedies
domestic laws fail to establish due process to protect violated rights
prohibition by the victim of access to domestic remedies or of exhaustion
unjustified delay in issuing a final decision on the case
the victim's situation of destitution in such a way that he cannot pay lawyers, and they are legally required without the State offering a free legal assistance service

The complaint must be filed within six months of the date of notification of the final court decision that exhausted domestic remedies. When it comes to the exception of exhaustion of domestic remedies, the six-month period does not apply, and must be submitted within a reasonable period.

Any person, group of persons or organization, on their own behalf or that of a third party, may submit petitions to denounce human rights violations against one or more OAS states. The Commission does not require the representation of a lawyer in the presentation and processing of the petition. The procedures are free, not depending on the payment of costs.

After the preliminary assessment, the Commission may

decide: (1) not to process the petition; (2) request additional information or documents; or (3) start processing.

When the petition enters the admissibility stage, it means that the necessary requirements for the Commission to study the petition have been met, but it does not necessarily imply a decision on the matter presented. In this case, the petition submitted will be sent to the State for its comments.

If the petition is accepted, the IACHR analyzes the parties' allegations and the evidence presented. At this stage, you can ask for more information, evidence and documents from the State and the petitioner and, if necessary, you can call a hearing or work meeting.

It is also a prerequisite for a petition to the IACHR to demonstrate inappropriate conduct (omissive or commissive) by the violating State, under penalty of non-admission. In this sense is Article 48 of the American Convention on Human Rights (Pact of San José of Costa Rica).

Before the international petition is presented, the violating State may neglect the victims' desires or even try to convince them that it is making every effort to repair the damage caused; the victim decides whether or not to report this leniency to international bodies. It should be noted that, in this propaedeutic phase, it is common for the governor to not even be one of the main actors, because, in view of the division of powers, it is up to the Judiciary to decide on judicial claims.

It is only with the petition presentation within the IACHR's scope that a friendly international settlement of the case becomes possible. It is possible to reach a consensual settlement with the State, depending on the will of the parties. It consists of negotiations to resolve the matter without having to complete the litigation process, under the supervision of the Commission. The main actors at that time become the ruler of the violating state and the victim (or his representative). It should be noted that the person who usually represents the violating State at the international level is the head of the Executive (or whoever determines it according to the country's maximum norm).

To exemplify, it is worth emphasizing that the Constitution of Brazil stipulates that the President of the Republic is competent to celebrate international acts on behalf of the Brazilian government (art. 84, VIII, of the 1988 Federal Constitution). The Minister of State for Foreign Affairs is responsible for "assisting the President of the Republic in formulating Brazil's foreign policy, ensuring its execution and maintaining relations with foreign states, international organizations and organizations" (Decree 2,246 / 97).

The ideal scenario is always a friendly solution, making it possible to equalize the victim's desire for reparation with the costs of the ruler. This would also be appropriate for the collaborative premises to which a humanitarian protection system must be linked. However, beforehand, it must be said that there is not such a disproportion of cases involving friendly (109)[8] and meritorious (98)[9] cases in the Inter-American Commission on Human Rights, which indicates that government officials do not always opt for the consensual solution.

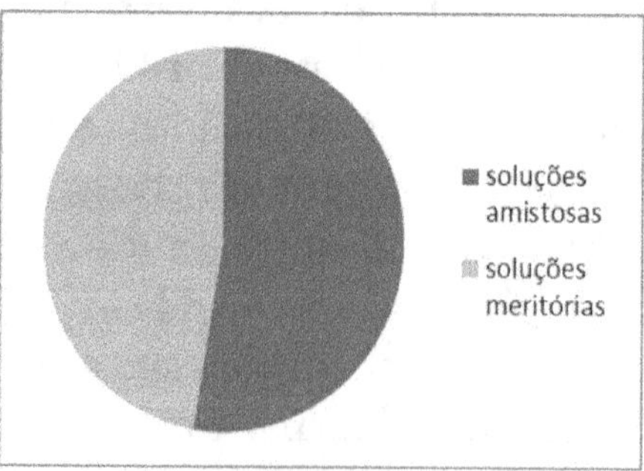

Still regarding this initial phase of the IACHR procedure, it should be noted that the role of the Commission is to approve any pact signed between the parties, provided that, obviously, the receipt of the petition has not been refused for offense to the regularity, legality and voluntariness. Therefore, in this phase, the IACHR does not act as a party directly involved, but it can be called upon to act in negotiation with a mediation function. This does not indicate that the Commission is a party to the agreement, but also, it cannot be thought that it does not function as a facilitator of the understanding process. It is worth noting that even the friendly decisions continue to be monitored by the IACHR, with a view to ascertaining whether all points of the agreement have been fully complied with by the violating country. Only in this case does such a case appear in the Commission's annual report with the status of fully complied with.

Since the case was not the subject of a friendly settlement, and after the initial petition was admitted, the Inter-American Commission on Human Rights proceeds to pursue the case under Article 48, then deciding the merits of the case, determining whether or not the State is responsible for violating human rights. The Commission issues a report on the merits, which may include recommendations to the State. When the State does not comply with the recommendations, the Commission may decide to: (1) publish the case; or (2) submit the case to the Inter-American Court, if it considers it.

It should be noted that it will always be possible to file the petition, even after the petition has been admitted. This is because, even though there was a judgment on the admissibility of the application, and despite the attempt to reach a friendly settlement of the case, the IACHR may have the case closed if the requirements for the continuation of the application are not present.

Finally, if it is not the case of archiving or agreement, the Commission will prepare a report, which will include recommendations to the violating State, under the terms of the ACHR:

Article 50.

1. If a solution is not reached, and within the period established by the Statute of the Commission, the Commission will draft a report in which it will present the facts and its conclusions. If the report does not represent, in whole or in part, the unanimous agreement of the members of the Commission, any of them may add their vote separately to that report. Verbal or written statements made by interested parties will also be

added to the report by virtue of item 1, and, of article 48.

2. The report will be forwarded to interested states, which will not be allowed to publish it.

3. When submitting the report, the Commission may formulate the proposals and recommendations it deems appropriate.

Article 51.

1. If, within three months, from the referral to the interested States of the Commission's report, the matter has not been resolved or submitted to the Court's decision by the Commission or the State concerned, accepting its competence, the Commission may issue, by the vote of the absolute majority of its members, their opinion and conclusions on the matter submitted for their consideration.

2. The Commission will make the pertinent recommendations and set a deadline within which the State must take the appropriate measures to remedy the situation examined.

3. After the deadline has elapsed, the Commission will decide, by the vote of an absolute majority of its members, whether or not the State has taken appropriate measures and whether or not to publish its report.

These recommendations are passed on secretly to the State party, and if the recommendations are not followed, the IACHR decides whether to publish such a demand in the annual case-follow-up report.

It can be seen, then, that the position of the IACHR only becomes privileged in the substantive recommendation phase (merit), since it is from there that the power of the governor and the victim to interfere in the substance of such unilateral decision of the Commission is reduced (as much as it is still possible for the parties to make an intercurrent agreement and give a new look to the worthy decision of the IACHR). Finally, the government official, upon receiving the decision of the Commission (merit), must decide whether to execute the recommendations.

It is important to mention that such recommendations are not endowed with true coercion, especially when looking at the prism of the possibility of imposing what has been determined, either on the basis of physical force or other sanctions (such as economic sanctions). In fact, there is no international body in the Inter-American Human Rights System that acts as a police corporation.

For this reason, if the recommendations are not met or what has been agreed was not fulfilled, it is possible to apply some measures provided for in the IACHR's rules (such as referral to the Inter-American Court) and the Organization of American States itself, in addition to political and economic retaliations. from other group member countries.[10] Nothing as serious as the expulsion of the bloc (as in the case of the European System) or even international war intervention.

In any case, after the recommendation was issued, the IACHR now monitors (and updates) the status of compliance with the measures that make up the solution in its annual follow-up reports: (1) fully complied, (2) partially complied with and (3) pending compliance (not met).

The repeated non-compliance with human rights brings as a punishment the express mention of this situation in the annual report sent by the Commission to the OAS General Assembly, pursuant to art. 59 of the Rules of Procedure of the Inter-American Commission on Human Rights.

It is important to underline that the Commission has no competence to assign individual responsibility, that is, it cannot determine whether a person is guilty or not. It can only determine the international responsibility of an OAS member state.

In seriousness and urgency cases, subject to compliance with certain requirements, the Commission may take precautionary measures, either on its own initiative or on request, to prevent irreparable damage to persons within its jurisdiction. Regardless of any case under evaluation, and with the possibility of periodic evaluation of the pertinence of maintaining the validity of the precautionary measures granted.

It should be noted that the Commission members' performance is independent and personal, not acting as representatives of their respective States, which favors a more advanced reading of IACHR's Statutes and Rules of Procedure.[11]

Finally, it should be noted that, even though the Commission plays a major role and may even issue recommendations, it still cannot be considered a jurisdictional body, but only an **almost jurisdictional** body.[12]

CHAPTER 2. THEORY OF RATIONAL DECISION

2.1. Rational decision theory

After reaching a minimum understanding of the rules and legal procedures within the framework of the IACHR, it becomes possible to establish the theoretical frameworks suitable for further investigation into the rational action of agents, especially with regard to the decisions of government officials in implementing solutions of human rights designed by the Commission.

The **rational decision-making model** has the ability to explain potential decisions made at the inter-American level. The main justification for using the rational decision assumption of the governor is that such a theoretical model is able to give homogeneity to the hypotheses (and the respective conclusions) in view of the analysis of costs and benefits carried out by the decision makers.

It is assumed that, among the various ways of deciding, agents have chosen to do so based on **rational strategies**[13], being important circumstances in this decision making some of the idiosyncrasies of the State to which they are linked (which were adopted as variables).

For this reason, the **rationality** of the agent's decision is not a hypothesis, but one of its **assumptions**, which ends up guaranteeing a final leveling between the most diverse governments in the countries that have cases mentioned in the follow-up report of the IACHR.

What allows homogenization of the decisions of the governors of Ecuador and the United States, for example, is the assumption of rational decision of both (*homo economicus*). If the calculating man is what is common in these examples, **context-**

ual factors (such as cultural, economic and political ones) work as the really **differentiating** circumstances of the different cases analyzed.

In this line of reasoning, what allows us to assume a certain **stability** in the **decisions** of several **governments** that succeed each other in the same country is that such internal factors of the countries do not usually change so much, remaining the restrictions and stimuli (imposed on the previous and subsequent governments) relatively stable. Political-electoral commitments and alliances may change, but the need to deal with contextual pressures remains constant.

Of course, government officials are not always able to see the problem in the same way. Roughly speaking, this is where the difference between the theory of **complete** rationality (downsian) and the theory of **limited** rationality (incomplete) comes from. If in the complete model the individual decides in an almost ideal world, in the theory of limited rationality the person acts with strong contextual and informational restrictions (leading not to the best decision in the abstract, but to the best possible deliberation in the specific case).

	Complete rationality (*downsian*)	Limited rationality (incompleta)
Amount of information and alternatives available	great (almost ideal world)	few (strong contextual and informational constraints)

It is inferred that people, when the matter is not trivial, act in the most **strategic** way possible making **expected utility calculations**. They make prospective judgments about which decision can guarantee them the **best results**, even if they don't always reach them. To be rational, in these terms, is not to be successful, but to **enhance your chances** by using more strategic and rational paths.

It is obvious that a model based on such premises is subject to criticism, because there are other explanatory theories. However, to ponder such disagreements, other punctually interesting **approaches** deserve to be used, like other **insti-**

tutionalist ones (ideational, syncretic, historical and socio-logical).

The worst criticisms may come from the fact that it is unlikely that all men will ever decide so calculatedly, especially in ordinary contexts. However, it is not assumed that people are all and always strategic. It can only be deduced that, in the context of very sophisticated arenas, as is the case with the relations established at the international level, the actors involved act rationally and seeking the **maximum possible advantage**.

Furthermore, any model based on rational decision is more an ordinary human conduct **approximate representation** than an undisputed reality. Thus, if the model of rational action does not always portray everyday reality, at least it will provide a fundamental explanation for the relations at the international level.

Even though not all men behave so rationally, the strategic and self-interested behaviors realization by a considerable part of individuals brings a certain rational **uniformity** to the group. Although unsophisticated individuals make uninformed decisions, the most informed will anticipate this conduct and compensate for it with a behavior conceived in exactly the opposite way. For example, if there is an excess of doctors, sophisticated individuals will become engineers and lawyers. In this way, the social result will approach the balance that would prevail if all the actors were sophisticated[14] In these terms, if one or other government official has decided to comply with an IACHR's solution based on luck (heads or tails, for example), this does not seem to be the usual rule of conduct.

Furthermore, it is necessary to understand that here we are not discussing human behavioral attributes (rationality intrinsic to each and every human being), but rather about the government officials' **decision-making process** and the reasons for the low rate of compliance with solutions proposed by the Commission.

Another criticism that could be directed to the present model concerns the impossibility of reducing the human participation interest in international deliberations on human rights to the political support maximization or the search for cost reduction.

In fact, there may be other reasons that move governments to comply with such determinations, such as altruism, prestige, respect, friendship and other social and psychological objectives. However, the rational man can maximize his advantages even when acting for an ethical purpose. The agent who builds a hospital can achieve a public purpose, but, concomitantly, achieve political prestige and religious satisfaction with such action. It is in this balance, in fact, that his expected ability is supported.

A good example of these other subjective costs may be the government's family group's opinion on an IACHR's specific recommendation success or failure. The present model does not include as one of the government's costs the risk of family prestige loss, although this is not averse to what was proposed by some collective action theory's sectarian. The search for the measurement of such subjective cost (in isolation) would bring great imprecision to the model that is being built here and, therefore, had been discarded.

> The possibility that, in a case where there is no economic incentive for an individual to contribute to the realization of a group interest, there may nevertheless be a social incentive for him to make his contribution must be considered. And it is obvious that it is a real possibility. If a small group of people members who had an interest in a collective benefit were also personal friends, or belonged to the same social club, and some members put the burden of providing that collective benefit on the back of others, they could, even if they gain something economically from this type of conduct, lose socially from it, and the social loss could weigh more on the balance than the economic gain. Your friends could use "social pressure" to get them to do their part in the process of achieving the group goal, under the threat of exclusion from the social club if they did not do it. These resources can be efficient, since daily observation shows that most people value their friends and colleagues company and look after their social status, social prestige and self-esteem.[15]

Finally, the present model uses the important vectors of limited rationality to ensure that a **logical line** is maintained. And it is this assumption's result that a **transitive list of preferences** is assumed for each of those involved in the international dispute. The fact is that this list is not overwhelming, as it depends on factors that influence the individual's decision-making ability. They are ideal types, like Max Weber used to invoke to promote an approximation between more generic and objective (scientific) concepts and the social agents' real action.

In addition, there are situations in which preferences are not even clear enough to allow gradation between them. It may be that some actors see some of the alternatives, others do not. To establish a gradation, it is necessary to first perceive such possibilities. This, in fact, is one of the most elementary limited rationality's principles. The **limited capacity principle** indicates that the human mind's ability to formulate and solve complex problems is very small compared to the size of the problems.[16]

For the theory of **limited rationality's** sectarian, in a context of limited information, complex problems, urgency in decision-making, as well as scarcity of resources, the rational government seeks the **best possible (satisfactory) result**, and not the truly maximizing result (truly great).

> Most human or individual decision-making decisions concern the satisfactory alternatives' discovery and selection; only in exceptional cases is the ideal alternatives' discovery and selection. To optimize the necessary processes, several magnitude orders are more complex than those needed to satisfy. An example is the difference between looking for a haystack to find the sharpest needle and looking for the haystack to find a needle sharp enough to sew. When making choices that meet satisfactory standards, the standards themselves are part of defining the situation.[17]

In this sense, it seems opportune to approach the **minimax strategy**, according to which, if there are circumstances in which an actor already knows he is predestined to lose the game, he is content to absorb the least possible impact. In this case, the other party involved (who will win) also needs to be content with just winning enough. The parties then force themselves to strike a certain balance[18].

Bringing these teachings to the model discussed here, it is possible to understand why there is a partially fulfilled solutions' prevalence in the IACHR cases' context. After all, the strategy in which the government elected to comply with some less costly measures (and on an emergency basis) would be **satisfactory**, aiming to escape the total defaulter of the solution's tainting status.

The government would not try to maximize its advantages to the extreme, but would only aim to get out of that emergency pressure situation with a different label than total noncompliant of the solution. On the other hand, the Commission would be content with this partial compliance, as it shows its victory in face of the Governor's tendency to not comply with any of the measures.

Hence, the IACHR leaves aside its intention to impose an even more disparaging label on the State, even though it would be possible to **push** the country to a higher level of compliance, if it publicly demonstrated its strategy through the disclosure of the measures' proportional compliance scale.

2.2. Institutions and organizational field

The main aspect of this study is the **government officials' decision** to comply or not with the IACHR's solutions, and not an IACHR and human rights standards' abstract structure observation. **The internal set of stimuli and limitations**[19] turns out to be more decisive than the international normative human rights discipline for the purposes of assessing whether or not the political authority will obey the Commission's recommendations. However, the fact that the main variables are related to the limitations intrinsic to the violating countries themselves does not totally rule out the Inter-American System set of rules' importance.

This set of formal and informal rules, principles, customs and beliefs that limit the agents' rational performance, disciplining how, when and within which beacons they can act, are called **institutions.** The concept of institutions for Political Science differs from Law, in wich they have the meaning of corporations (organs).

> Institutions, seen as the organizing principles of interaction, can be simply defined as rules of the game (North, 1990, p. 3) in a society and can be formal or informal. These rules serve as traffic guides for the flow and transactions of goods (material and symbolic) between actors, including individuals and organizations. (...) Institutions are cultural and not scientific, because they do not require logical or empirical evidence or appreciate forgery. These rules create favorable values for actions and interactions in the forms of morality, faith, ideology, decency or ability (to heal and execute).[20]

Realize that the agents and the rules of the game are not in a vacuum, but in an **organizational field**, which translates the dimensional sphere where the interactions between agencies (individuals and organizations) and institutions occur. This organizational field consists of a common activity context, in which corporations and individuals are subject to the same rules.

> When organizations and individuals submit to similar institutions, they are said to be in an institutional field (Lin, 1994b). Within an institutional field, actors (including individuals, networks and organizations) recognize, demonstrate and share rituals and behaviors, and sign restrictions and incentives, as determined by social institutions.[21]

Institutions	Organizational field
A set of formal and informal rules, principles, customs and beliefs that limit the agents' rational performance of agents, disciplining how, when and within which goals they can act.	Dimensional sphere where interactions between agencies (individuals and organizations) and institutions take place. It consists of a *common activity context*, in which corporations and individuals are subject to the same rules.

The first (and most important) institutions are those that are placed internally in the countries themselves, like the Constitution, ordinary laws, complementary laws and rules of political conduct in general. Regarding transnational regulations, the main one is the American Convention on Human Rights (also called the San José Pact of Costa Rica), without departing from other diplomas of humanitarian interest derived from or that have inspired it.

The very interaction between the IACHR and states parties, in the continuous game of the Convention application in practical cases, ends up creating informal rules between them. These are called **structuring-structures**,[22] since such legal relations have the capacity not only to strengthen the application of the rules already in force, but also to build other standards to be followed by that community.

It cannot be ruled out that the **invisible rules** that guide the almost homogeneous construction of the IACHR's solutions are institutions built over the years. For this reason, the way of acting and designing public policies - which seems to be crystallizing in the inter-American human rights context - indicates the existence of **informal patterns** that have been outlined during the continuous rounds between the Commission and the violating states. Such standards are supported by solid ideas of humanitarian protection, which works as a **cognitive lock** that rejects any attempt to change these formulas for building solutions.

The belief that there is a need for formal rigor in decisions can be anchored in principle that *with human rights there is no negotiation or dialogue*, a hypothesis that may explain the system ineffectiveness' partial degree. This premise is important and is related to ideational institutionalism, which is not completely opposed to rationalist precepts.

In **ideational institutionalism**, ideas are treated as resources that serve as cognitive blocks, models or weapons in distributive struggles (for money or power, illustratively) in a possible new institutional arrangement. Ideas give institutions coherence, shielding them from attempts at mutations, or, on the contrary, are used as weapons against rules that become unwanted. In other words, the ideas hinder the agents' freedom to act in the face of their desire for change, as well as facilitating the destruction of the structures put in place.

> Ideas are the speech's substantive content. (...) **Speech** is the interactive process of transmitting **ideas**. (...) The discursive institutionalism institutions, moreover, are not external structures-of-following-the-rules but simultaneously internal structures and constructs for agents whose "background ideational skills" within a given "meaning context" explain how institutions are created, exist and whose "foreground discursive skills", following a "communication logic", explain how institutions change or persist.[23]

Clear indication of this ideological adjustment of performance's relevance is that the Inter-American Commission on Human Rights was created in 1959 and, in the decades immediately following its genesis, it was forced to act more acidly in face of violating countries.

> The IACHR conducts country studies and examines thematic issues of regional interest. During the 1970s and 1980s, the commission was particularly aggressive in using its independent authority to pressure repressive governments. His reports on Chile under the military regime were particularly important for domestic and international human rights defenders. As the general human rights situation in the region has improved in the post-Cold War world, the Commission's reports have become less prominent, but remain significant. For example, the commission issued two reports on Bolivia in 2005 and reports on Honduras in 2009 and 2010 that helped to draw attention to serious problems in those countries and, in late 2009, published an important report on citizen security and human rights.[24]

2.3. Agencies

It is necessary to demystify the idea that only a natural person can be an agent. The present model is not compatible with such limitation. Like rationalist models based on game theory, corporations not only have the ability to influence other agencies' performance, but also, in this case, can be considered involved parties. It is not necessary for the player to be an individual: it can be a **team**, **company** or **nation**. Any group that has common interests regarding the game is considered as a single player.[25]

Adopting **organizations** as this system's agencies is extremely useful, as it allows them to clarify their **intrinsic purposes**, demonstrating their own ability to guide actions and strategies **autonomously** in relation to their members or members. There is no denying that corporations cannot achieve their goals without the material assistance of human beings; however, this does not prevent it from being considered a **singular entity** and with different desires than those of its members.

When forming organizations, individuals give up part of their individual rights of action in the organization's favor. They become part of the corporation's action, following its standards and instructions, rather than pursuing only its most immediate goals. The organization itself becomes an agent that makes rational decisions, pursuing its own interests, trying to maximize its gains and minimize its costs. There is nothing mysterious about it; the corporate actor is guided by senior executives or the board of directors, but they do not act as individuals who pursue only their private interests; generally, senior executives or leaders play a role in encouraging others to do what they consider to be in the organization's interest. This corporate identity is encouraged by modern Western law, which recognizes the corporation as a legal person, as a kind of fictitious individual who has the right to own and to transact with other individuals in society.[26]

The **designs** and **objectives** are the organization's, and not the human being's who is the material executor of such missions. It must be recognized that organizations have their own **logic and interests** as a unified body, which does not prevent their members from having their own ambitions.

There is some resistance in accepting an organization as an agency, as it is argued that, as there are usually multiple individual interests involved in the group context, there would be finalistic dispersion. In this case, there would be so many purposes that, due to its great vectorization, it would be very difficult to characterize objectives and own interests.

Despite the coherence of this argument, it must be emphasized that the specialized literature argues that **fragmentation** is not a **corporations'** characteristic alone. The rational **man** himself is also the result of his own finalistic division, for example between reason and passion; it is this dialectic between reason and human emotions that allows one part to prevail over the other. Therefore, it does not matter if there are many **different wills** in an organization, it is enough to overcome such supposed anarchy, that there is one that **prevails**. Both the individual and the collectivity are divided rather than unitary. The party in charge can exercise far-reaching planning to restrict the nearsighted or impulsive other parties' action.[27]

Along these lines, it is possible to consider the Inter-American **Commission** on Human Rights as one of the **main actors** at the international level. It is noted that there are IACHR's main purposes including the desire that its recommendations be carried out by the states, as well as seeing the Inter-American Human Rights System function properly and strengthen itself in the regional context of defending human rights.

See what advocates OAS Resolution 447, which establishes the Statute of the Inter-American Commission on Human Rights:

> **Article 18.** The Commission has the following tasks with respect to the member states of the Organization:
>
> a) to stimulate human rights awareness among the peoples of America;
>
> b) make recommendations to the states' governments to adopt progressive measures in favor of human rights, within the scope of their legislation, constitutional precepts and international commitments, as well as appropriate provisions to promote respect for those rights.

The central point is that the IACHR is an organization composed by a small number of voting members.

This makes it easier to achieve and show more homogeneous (less fragmentary) decisions and purposes for such a collegiate. Perhaps if it were an organ composed by a much larger number of people, this presumption could be weakened.

Mentioned by the IACHR as one of the agencies, it is necessary to focus on the **violating state's ruler**, but with a different perspective. This is because, regardless that the demands are proposed to the State's disadvantage (and not the government's), one chooses not to recognize the State as an agency, since the fragmentation of interests within a State is much more profound than it is in relation to the IACHR. The state is divided into several powers and thousands of organs; there are so many idiosyncratic interests that it becomes much less visible the prevalence of one over others.

In addition, it is the governor (Head of Government or Head of State) who is usually tasked by local Constitutions to represent the State in international dealings, either directly or through an intermediary person or corporation. It is up to him, then, to make his political will prevail (or to convince them of the adequacy of what he proposes) in face of possible other conflicting positions internally. This can be seen even from the Vienna Convention on the Law of Treaties.[29]

Another important point is that the governor, as the maximum representative of the State's interest in the international path, also ends up protecting his own when choosing to adopt humanitarian public policies. After all, a government official loses the possibility of remaining in power if he is not skilled enough to maintain credibility with voters and also his prestige at the international level. Therefore, it makes much more sense to have the ruler as the central actor since he is the most interested in harmonizing all the diverse interests in the bowels of the country he represents. That is why it is said that the **ruler's** figure is **triple-faced**, as he needs to compose interests of the various powers of the State (internal **bureaucratic** facet), please national voters **(electoral** facet) and, in addition, he needs to maintain adequate diplomatic relations with countries and international organizations that may favor you in some way (**transnational** aspect).

Finally, there is still the **victim** of the violation (or whoever does it sometimes). Such an agency can be represented by a person or even by an organization. It is perfectly possible, as said, to appear as a petitioner as a legal entity (such as an association or foundation), but always depending on the previous existence of a humanitarian violation human victim.

Even though the victim's role is less important in this analytical approach, the rational action assumption indicates that she also wants to strengthen the bodies and institutions that govern human relations in the IACHR context. After all, a healthy regional humanitarian system is able to prevent other similar violations from happening again in face of it or others in a similar situation.

Main agencies of the Inter-American Human Rights System		
Inter-American Commission on Human Rights	Violating state's ruler	Violation victing

2.4. Limitations to choices

It is assumed that everyone involved in this context is rational and, therefore, liable to make optimal choices. There are optimal options when everyone involved in the international dispute chooses the best strategies in order to increase their individual advantages. However, this is not always possible, as the rules may **limit the choice of the best solution**, leaving only a few less desirable alternatives.

To better understand this limitation, it is necessary to imagine a **two-bladed scissors**. According to such an analogy, the true decision-making set can only be understood if the **context blade** and the **rational capacity blade** are taken into account together.[30]

Many of the government's problems of loss of legitimacy center on the inability to provide a perfect solution to the problems presented to him; although this does not indicate that they are irrational or unwary to the point of not seeing all the alternatives that were possible for them.

In this sense, it seems appropriate to also think about public humanitarian policies taking into account the **internal and international influences** that agents suffer. This is a consolidated trend, and it is not appropriate to understand countries as hermetic political units. Policy making is a domestic affair that involves national governments and their citizens. However, the international system is also increasingly vital in shaping domestic public policy choices.[31]

However, this does not indicate that forcibly applying a successful humanitarian public policy design in another country will achieve equal success in all other countries in the bloc.

Another point to be highlighted is that, when everyone involved plays individually and strategically, this can end up making it difficult to achieve really great global results. "The collective action problems because it is difficult to get people to cooperate for their mutual benefit".[32]

The governor (whatever the time or the situation experienced internally) decides for the adoption of an international agreement or recommendation based on the burdens and bonuses weighing, regardless of the future effects that this may cause in the local and external scope.

Therefore, one of the hypotheses is that the repeated non-compliance with public policies, within the IACHR's scope, is motivated by the government's rational recalcitrance in the face of the high costs imposed because of the inadequate designs of public policies carried out within the Commission's scope.

This precludes the thesis that government officials are allowing human rights violations in their territories (due to the failure to implement measures that prevent the repetition of similar acts) to reopen an international dialogue with regional protection bodies.

The overriding reason why government officials are not fully complying with the measures may be due to the inadequacy of the proposed (or even agreed) public policy designs. Therefore, focus should be given to the presumed implementation costs, represented by numerous variables, among them the solution designs' complexity.

2.5. Game theory and iterative good faith

Most of the countries that make up the Organization of American States (OAS) have more than one petition in their disagreement, being processed by the Inter-American Commission on Human Rights. This can be seen when analyzing the IACHR's case follow-up report.

Even those countries that currently have only one case processing in Commission, it must be emphasized that other existing demands may not yet be included in the follow-up report. Furthermore, it is always possible for new violation reports to be filed against him in the IACHR and, therefore, be obliged to participate in a new international dispute.

This information is of paramount importance as it indicates the propensity that those involved (mainly the Commission and the government) will find themselves in other similar international disturbs. In the context of **game theory**, these occurrences can be considered as **iterative** games (those that usually repeat themselves), which makes it possible for players to learn from previous rounds.

In these iterative disputes' context, those involved in these multiple cases can learn from the past strategies adopted by other actors in international demand and, therefore, start adapting to others' the future behavior. Depending on the actors' form of action, there may be the creation of a greater or lesser trust environment between them, which would be permeated by what is called iterative good faith.

This learning procedure is not a specificity restricted to game theory sectarians, nor is it a peculiarity restricted to human beings; even the so-called irrational animals decide using informational shortcuts, the so-called heuristic[33]. It is a fact that this capacity for human learning is even greater than that of other living beings, especially when acting in a context of greater sophistication. The study of this learning process is allocated by **behavioral** theorists in the **learning theory** context.[34]

Well, based on the assumption that continuous rounds can occur, if the actors involved in the international dispute act in an extremely individualistic way, or even if they act in an erratic way, it is possible to create an environment of distrust among those involved in future cases that they link up again. On the other hand, if the strategies adopted by the players are collaborative and predictable, an environment of greater reliability will be built between the actors, when in similar and successive contexts.

Game theory and iterative good faith
repetitive events (iterative games)
creating an environment of greater or lesser trust and collaboration
learning from past strategies (law of effect and theory of learning)

In general, game theory experts agree that **cooperation** becomes easier when players participate in **games that repeat itself**, so that the deserter is punished in successive rounds. There are other conditions inherent in the game itself that can favor cooperation, for example, limited number of players, abundant information about each player's past behavior, and the fact that the future is not overly discounted by players.[35]

It is in this context that it seems logical to argue that rationality should not be used only to explain a player's strategic action, but also to correct it in the face of the risks of his current and future decision-making selfishness. It is in this pattern recognition process that repetitive good faith produces an cooperation environment, but it also punishes negative behavior by those who act at the expense of collaborative premises.

In fact, the biggest problem with these inter-American iterative games is that the State's **failure to comply** with the previous solution may be **impacting** the design of a later solution by the IACHR; the Commission can try to punish the violating state with an even more complex design than the previous one. Even if there is such organizational retaliation, this does not seem to be enough to encourage further compliments. Actually, it is estimated that it is much more likely that there will be further non-compliance. In fact, the formally adequate the IACHR's design can contribute much more to States' decision to fully comply with solutions, even if there have been previous non-compliances.

After all, if the drawings are made contrary to the States' contextual realities, even if in response to previous non-compliances, the government would be given the perfect justification for not complying with the next drawings presented to them. If this is really happening, the IACHR itself may be involuntarily contributing to a less alkaline environment construction.

Furthermore, this iterative good faith reasoning applies both in the context of **meritorious** solutions and in the search for **friendly** means of resolving the demand. If the parties do so in good faith, it is guaranteed that those who do so are seen more favorably than those who do not. In that case, it matters little whether the game will be fought in face of the same victim or others; it is important to know that the behavior of States will be predictable and accessible to other possible participants in the context.

If the drawings are adequate and the good faith conditions are installed, but still a government official seeks the friendly solution only as a subterfuge for not submitting the demand to the decision on the merits, he may even obtain a momentary advantage, but he needs to suffer the consequences. In the long run, an environment of discredit will emerge because of new locked rounds (iterative rounds) involving such a ruler. In the same spot is the governor who is reluctant to not fulfill balanced meritorious solutions.

These are pseudocooperation negative effects, which makes it even more interesting to create a scoring countries ranking to the compliance degree with the case solutions, since the effects of this label can affect eventual relations between countries, which seems to be a consequence that violating countries tend to fear.

2.6. Agent preferences

There may be multiple feelings or purposes that permeate the strategies adopted by the actors involved in the international demand (Commission, government and victim). However, these other purposes and desires do not make up the predominant picture of these agents 'typical characteristics.

In this context, there are specific and ideal purposes for each of the actors in the Inter-American Human Rights System's context, as well as a common purpose for those involved.

The **common purpose** concerns the intention that everyone has to see the Inter-American Human Rights System work properly and strengthen itself in the regional context of defending human rights (an objective that is even expressly included in some friendly solutions).

Of course that this common purpose can be made compatible with each party's particular interests. Proof of this is that most of the countries that make up the Organization of American States voluntarily adhered to the San José da Costa Rita Pact (American Convention on Human Rights).

Attention is drawn to the countries that repeatedly violate human rights 'hypothetical incongruity if they voluntarily link themselves to international control bodies, especially countries with less robust GDPs. But that is not quite what we see in practice. Few are the countries that permanently deviate from these international heterocontrols. This shows that the **label of adherence** to the system is something that truly matters to member countries, which needs to be better explored by the IACHR.

The general rule is that countries with more limited budgets and, therefore, more likely to be unable to bear the costs of complying with the Commission's recommendations, adhere (with or without reservations) in the same way as the others; incredible as it may seem, the richest seem to resist adherence even a little more. This can show that the adhesion label is something even more important for countries that seek to consolidate themselves in some way on the international stage.

Below, the list of countries that have cases in the IACHR's follow-up report and their degree of attachment to the inter-American system:

**Chart 1 - Adherence to the mechanisms of the
Inter-American Human Rights System** [36]

Country	Adherence to the Regional System (American Convention on Human Rights)	Voluntary submission to the Inter-American Court of Human Rights (Article 62)	Adherence to the contentious bias of the Inter-American Commission on Human Rights (Article 45)
Antigua and Barbuda			
Argentina	X	X	X
Bahamas			
Barbados	X	X	
Belize			
Bolívia	X	X	
Brazil	X	X	
Canada			
Chile	X	X	X
Colombia	X	X	X
Cuba			
El Salvador	X	X	
Ecuador	X	X	X
United States of America			
Grenada	X		
Guatemala	X	X	
Guyana			
Haiti	X	X	
Honduras	X	X	
Jamaica	X		X
Mexico	X	X	
Nicaragua	X	X	X
Paraguay	X	X	
Peru	X	X	X
Dominican Republic	X	X	

Country	Adherence to the Regional System (American Convention on Human Rights)	Voluntary submission to the Inter-American Court of Human Rights (Article 62)	Adherence to the contentious bias of the Inter-American Commission on Human Rights (Article 45)
Saint Kitts and Nevis			
Saint Lucia			
Saint Vincent and the Grenadines			
Suriname	X	X	
Trinidad and Tobago	X	X	
Uruguay	X	X	X
Venezuela	X	X	X

Another possible justification for so many formal adhesions to the regional system is the existence of **positive diffusion** among nations, creating a wave of stimulus in which close and similar countries feel sensitized to adhere to the humanitarian protection mechanisms. Such a conglomerate complete jettisoning could be interpreted internally as the national governor's lack of ability.

Anyway, when they come together, the countries start to form a supranational entity, which, then, starts to enjoy autonomy before the member countries and, better, with its own purposess.

The **common purpose** concerns the intention that everyone has to see the inter-American human rights protection system work properly and strengthen itself in the regional context for the defense of human rights (an objective that even expressly appears in some friendly solutions).

Common purpose
See the Inter-American Human Rights System function properly and strengthen in the regional context for the human rights defense

It is assumed that the IACHR's main purpose is to reaffirm its importance in the regional context, as well as to guarantee the effectiveness of the system (including with the fulfillment of its solutions). To achieve this goal, **an Inter-American Com-**

mission on Human Rights transitive list of preferences is assumed: 1) the violation is resolved, in full, in the atria of the violating country itself; 2) if the dispute is not resolved nationally and the international dispute is presented, be resolved in full by friendly means; 3) if the international dispute is not resolved amicably, that it be solved entirely in the meritorious way; 4) if the international dispute is not resolved in full, unless it is partially resolved (through a friendly or meritorious way); 5) if the international dispute is not resolved, neither totally nor partially, that the violating State be reprimanded by the competent bodies.

Preferences of the Inter-American Commission on Human Rights
1) the violation is fully resolved in the atria of the violating country
2) if the dispute is not resolved nationally and the international dispute is presented, be resolved in full by friendly means
3) if the international dispute is not resolved amicably, that it be solved entirely in the meritorious way
4) if the international dispute is not resolved in full, at least that is partially resolved (through friendly or meritorious means)
5) if the international dispute is not resolved, neither totally nor partially, that the violating State is reprimanded by the competent bodies

Regarding the governors (representing the respective violating state), it can be said that they (ideally) seek not to be demanded internationally; however, if they are, they aim, at the lowest possible cost, **to solve such international demands without their internal support being shaken and good international relations being put in check**. After all, the risk of losing prestige (internal and external) compromises its maintenance in power. This is presumed to be the elemental driving force of such an agent.

The legal, economic, institutional and political cost matters a lot in this rational decision on the adoption of such measures. **The governor plays in multiple arenas and tries to equalize, based on the rules and norms set, personal, collective and corporate interests.** After all, the government official does not want to lose internal support (by undertaking public policies that do not guarantee the political support maintenance or obtainment), nor does he wish to see himself at international risk because he is not fulfilling the human rights preservation universal imperative.

In addition, the violating state's governor appears to be unwilling to bear the costs of a very complex public policy, unless he can derive sufficient benefits from it. For that, it is necessary to assume a transitive list of **violating States' governors preferences**, when the focus is on an human rights violation that can be assessed in the Inter-American Human Rights System: 1) they do not see any human rights violations accusations being sent to the Inter-American Human Rights System; 2) if the demand is presented and accepted by the IACHR, resolve it in whole or in part, either by consensual or meritorious means, provided that its costs are never greater than its benefits; 3) to resolve, totally or partially, the international dispute presented to the IACHR, either by consensual means or by meritorious means, provided that he loses less than he could lose (*minimax* scenario).

Preferences of the violating states' rulers
1) to not see any human rights violations accusations being sent to the Inter-American Human Rights System
2) if the demand is presented and accepted by the IACHR, resolve it in whole or in part, either by consensual or meritorious means, provided that its costs are never greater than its benefits
3) to resolve, totally or partially, the international dispute presented to the IACHR, either by consensual means or by meritorious means, provided that he loses less than he could lose (*minimax* scenario)

Finally, the **violations victims** (or their representatives) seek to have their wishes for reparation met, either in the internal orbit or, in the case of petition filing to the IACHR, by a satisfactory international solution (friendly or meritorious).

Based on the assumption that the victims' primary intention is to see themselves assisted in their reparatory efforts and, by ricochet, to ensure that the Inter-American System is effective, the list of **victims' preferences** (and their representatives) should be mentioned.: 1) to receive, fully and promptly, the moral and material reparations at the national level; 2) receive, in full, moral and material reparations in face of a friendly agreement or merit settlement; 3) partially receive material and moral reparations, because of the perpetrated violation, due to a friendly agreement or a meritorious solution.

Violations victims' preferences
1) to receive, fully and promptly, the moral and material reparations at the national level
2) receive, in full, moral and material reparations in face of a friendly agreement or merit settlement
3) partially receive material and moral reparations, because of the perpetrated violation, due to a friendly agreement or a meritorious solution.

It should be noted that, although the present model brings several lists of agents and organizations' preferences focused on the present context (IACHR, government and victim), they are not expected to always opt for the most maximizing alternatives. Not that there is a transitive list of preferences, that is, an order of these desires. **The ordering exists, but there may be an observer's perception error** (who cannot see all the arenas in which the decision-maker is involved) **or the perception error is from the decision-maker himself** (who does not clearly see the best possible solution in the specific case).

This distortion to the ideal preferences cited does not mean that their action is considered irrational, but that **it may be restricted to contingencies and limitations typical of the theory of limited rationality.** Furthermore, the hidden arenas may give the false perception that the ruler did not choose the best alternative, being that, in fact, he chose what was possible for him.

The ruler may not be able to afford the costs of all measures; it may also not have the internal legal conditions to implement a certain measure; moreover, he could think that he would lose his political support if he dislocated funds from an important social path to make a project for prisoners in the prison system, for example.

What is not explicitly assumed here is that men have complete information, that they have no social commitments that restrict their alternatives, that their preferences are entirely consistent or remain constant, or that they pursue a specific end goal to the exclusion of all others. These more restrictive assumptions, which are not made in the present analysis, characterize rationalist models of human conduct, such as that of game theory.[37]

Defining the decision's rationality depends on the **contextual analysis** in which the rational decision maker is involved. For this reason, it is recommended that the governor regularly sees himself impelled to situations that demand a quick decision (even with serious informational restrictions), which has the ability to prevent his eyes from turning to the most optimizing alternative, forcing him to adopt the best possible solution for that context, which is called a **satisfactory alternative.**

CHAPTER 3. COSTS OF IMPLEMENTING IACHR SOLUTIONS

3.1. Internal limitations to external solutions

Costs relate to contingent or historical **limitations** that influence the ruler's decision to implement or not a specific public policy agreed or recommended within the IACHR's scope. Such costs were divided into four categories: economic, institutional, legal and political.

This costs separation in various categories arises from the didactic option, due to the need of highlighting the predominant characteristic of each political and social intervention genre: **wealth, structural organization, power of command and information**.

While budgetary costs are relevant, as the world is experiencing an austerity crisis, it is not only those with an economic bias that will be addressed; in fact, money does matter, but that is not enough to explain the non-compliance phenomenon with agreed or recommended measures.

For example, regarding the decision making political factors, if the countries' budget is directed towards public policies restricted to the human rights violations' arena (determined within the international organizations' scope), it is possible that **local governments will not be able to honor other electoral commitments** and therefore lose internal legitimacy. This shows that political discredit can play an important role even greater than money.

Voters, when they do not see the projects listed in the government plans being fulfilled, can turn against their leaders, causing a potential responsiveness crisis. The government needs to balance its efforts, therefore, in order to **reconcile its people's interests, equalizing external and internal pressures**.

In the rational action model, government officials are aware of these risks and will work to avoid these obstacles.

> At the transnational level, the challenges to democracy on the inputs side arise from the need to adapt the conceptions and practices developed at the national level to a reality in which transnational actors and global events are increasingly influential. Democracy's normative conceptions and empirical implementations developed in and about the nation-state are not easily applied at the supranational level, with regard to political institutions and civil society. In fact, 'democracy as we know it within countries does not exist in a Globalized Space. (...) In short, the movements in neoliberal post-democracies face a political institutions' responsibility crisis.[38]

The ruler, therefore, has to be skilled enough to be able to manage the limited budget in such a way as to honor the interest of voters favorable to his holding on to power and gain the greatest possible number of votes from those who did not previously support him. For this reason, humanitarian public policies - which are not always able to generate such a political consensus - **may suffer political resistance from the government and the constituency that supports it.**

> According to the economic theory of democracy, governments never undertake any policy unless they hope to win votes (or at least not lose votes) in doing so. Therefore, for every citizen who opposes a particular act, there are other citizens favorable to it. (...) Looking at the whole complex of its acts between elections, the governing party feels that including this act wins more votes than excluding it. The party can afford to offend some voters with this act because they are the minority towards him, their feelings against him are not as intense as the feelings of those favorable to him.[39]

Every humanitarian public policy has a price to be paid and, interestingly, the nominal value of any *indemnity* is not always the most important in the government's decision making. The bargains that may need to be made in order to pass a law are even more impeding than monetary reparation payment would be. Hence, **voters' perception that government time and energy is being spent on agendas that are not correlated to it, can lead**

to legitimacy crises.

In this restriction and costs divided into several arenas scenario, it remains for the government to know how many chips to bet (and how much of its prestige to test) to see an IACHR's public policy implemented. Remember that, for this model, government analysis about the burdens and bonuses of implementing a recommended or agreed public policy within the Commission is a matter of survival and maintaining legitimacy.

The fact is that the governors do not accept that their project of governance and power is unsuccessful **due to the excessively costly impositions of solutions coming from an international organ**, mainly because the IACHR does not even need to account for its actions internally.

3.2. Economic costs

Among the various costs that must be taken into account by the governments involved in the present inter-American laws are the presumed economic costs. It is worth recalling that all rights have costs and, of course, as well as the measures recommended or agreed within the IACHR's scope.[40]

There is a clear link between fiscal capacity and the ability to implement public policies.

> In any case, the state has (...) limits on its fiscal potential. These vary considerably in each specific case according to the country's wealth or poverty, the concrete details of its national and social structure, and nature. of your wealth. (...) They can also differ according to the military expenditures or debt service's extent, their bureaucracy's power and morality and the intensity of their people's "state awareness".[41]

The State only works because of the economic and financial resources raised from the people who are part of that nation, and it is possible to say that rights only exist where there is a budget that allows it. It is worth noting that **many rights have both positive and negative dimensions**,[42] as the right to health, considering that the State must not affect the integrity of people (refraining from polluting) and at the same time is obliged to take care of the citizens 'health (delivering medical services to prevent and cure diseases).

Despite the foregoing, the economic cost of paying indemnities, unlike what one might think, is not always the most impactful in the decision-making context[43], which is probably the lowest cost for States. So much so that this is one of the measures with the highest rate of compliance, and it may be seen as a fair, punctual and low-cost palliative about a mistake perpetrated by the State. Therefore, it is necessary to pay attention to the most substantive costs in the face of humanitarian public policies indicated in the IACHR's case solutions, and not to specific indemnities..

Furthermore, it cannot be overlooked that government officials prioritize expenditures that are perceived by voters and can generate political dividends in elections, and do not necessarily invest in the greatest benefits for people.

> The government gives voters what they want, not necessarily what benefits them. As long as citizens know what benefits them, there should be no difference between the real budget and the "right" budget. But if there are benefits that government spending would produce that people are not aware of, the government will not spend money to produce it, unless it believes it can make it known before the next elections. For the government is mainly interested in people's votes, not their well-being, and it will not increase their well-being if it costs votes. And it would lose votes if it increased taxes or inflation - which people are aware of - to produce benefits that people are not aware of. Many citizens would shift their votes to some other party that would only produce more tangible benefits at a lower total cost - even if they were in fact worse off under that party.[44]

In this context, even if economic resources were not scarce, it does not seem to matter to the government if it was advisable to ensure compliance with international humanitarian recommendations, even if considered good actions for society and able to bring well-being to the group. In fact, the relationship that is outlined here is more political-electoral than economic: **give people what they want (as far as they can give),**

not what will be good for them.

This scenery may stem from the difficulty of convincing the certain countries' populations about the importance of internalizing certain public policies, such as those that guarantee more dignified conditions in their prisoners' treatment.

Some of the more **traditional neo-liberalism sectarians'** position is even worse; for them, governments that are guided by public policy planning (Keynesianism) are seen as individual **freedoms' invaders**. Only people would know how to define what they really want, and the State, when it tries to do so, does so at the expense of people's freedom (Hayek, 1976, p. 42).

Even if it is assumed that the governor will seek to please his constituency (and not necessarily do what is good), there will still be clashes of interest among the local population. This is because, against a background of budgetary scarcity, the task of determining which public policies should be implemented is difficult, since voters tend to be interested in varied and not always coincident objects.

> In the real world, people's preference ratings are not identical (...). Although almost every man agrees with most of his colleagues on some policies, he is also in the minority on others. It is these "rotating majorities"'s presence that prevents men from reaching equilibrium with governments. The government must implement a complex combination of many policies, some pleasing a majority, some pleasing the other majority, and some pleasing only a minority with intense feelings about them. It can afford to undertake policies favored only by a minority because it does not stand or fall into any issue, but in the mix as a whole.[45]

It is essential to understand that all of these recommended public policies must be funded by the same funds source: the budget. Not only them, but also any and all State expenses, such as a physical structure construction, government employee remuneration and the basic public services functioning (health and safety, for example).

This perception by national voters that everyone has the right to take some particular advantage of the money that is in the common-pool resource ends up driving the government official (who is unable to carry out this budget juggling) to aim for the most general public policies possible.

It doesn't matter how selfish it may seem; each group wants its share of interests guaranteed by that public funding source. Understanding the link between economic costs and political costs is essential for understanding this dilemma.

This all leads to the **tragedy of the commons**, that is, a situation in which individuals, acting independently, selfish and uncoordinated, end up producing effects contrary to the community interests, exhausting some type of common resource.

It is a specific type of tragedy of the commons: the **pseudodemocratic**. We explain. Under the need to meet the agenda of more general and democratic interests label, more powerful groups are able, politically, to prevent the public policies construction that do not favor them so directly, moving away from the human rights protection system's cooperative character. Hence, poorly designed public policies can be the barricade used to stop the resources spending on IACHR's solutions.

And these broader preferences can encourage natural antipathies to the agenda generated by some of the public human rights policies, which, as a rule, are very specific and aimed at a small (minority) group of people (political prisoners, prisoners, police violence victims, Indians, women, people with disabilities, etc.). This voter resistance presumption seems to be much more typical in not so free governments.

In this context, the reductionist discourse that the government would be facing a Sophie's choice seems useful to strengthen internal resistance to the fulfillment of the IACHR's solutions: either the money is spent to meet the national population's basic desires or the Commission's solutions are accepted, which would only benefit marginalized groups.

> The speech contributes to the success or failure of ideas first by how it articulates its substantive content. What makes a speech successful, in fact, includes several of the same things that make ideas successful: relevance to the topics under dis-

The fact is that the argument about draining money (which could be used in an hospital construction, for example) to implement public policy (due to abusive violations by police at the prisoners 'expense, illustratively) can lead to the rulers loss of internal political support.

The desire for the vote of electors' the most diverse groups (due to the increase in democratic pillars in most countries) creates an environment conducive to pressure from various groups of voters to bar humanitarian public policies acceptance.

This whole discussion has a practical importance, especially in face of the variable choice regarding the political regime's degree of freedom. The freer a regime is, it is assumed that the lower its resistance and antagonism to the humanitarian agenda, even if it comes from a transnational organization and even though the design is not so adequately formatted.

One cannot forget, in the same way, that international bodies are not endowed with the same political responsiveness as government officials. By failing to take responsibility for the economic and social impacts of their decisions in the violating country's domestic sphere, supranational bodies end up affecting the governments 'commitments with the citizens 'wishes (voters) in complex solutions' design, colliding with the intentions of self-interested government officials.

Therefore, in the complex process of forming a public policy, its final intention will only be achieved if the decision is in accordance with a synthesis of the conflicting arguments between the parties involved (which is close to syncretic institutionalism). This is even the key to the post-positivist bias, which comes to mitigate the purely positivist analysis rigors.

Post-positivist analyzes' most important point is that they are sensitive to the confused or chaotic realities of the public policy process, unlike their positivist counterparts, which tend to have an orderly, even mechanistic, conception of the politics realm. For positivists, political problems are largely technical issues that can be dealt with effectively as soon as the right solution is found through rigorous technical analysis. On the other hand, pospositivists correctly point out that technical analysis needs to be complemented by studying a range of other factors, including conflicts arising from different values and interests.[47]

In short, when the international body limits itself to imposing complex solutions and composed by measures that are difficult to comply with, it promotes the government officals' autonomy restriction speech in the management of these already so limited resources in the *common pool*, increasing the chances that these measures are seen internally as exogenous budget violations. Freer governments tend to overcome these difficulties and better manage such dilemmas; the less free may react not so collaboratively and use arguments to legitimize their internal decision not to comply with the measures.

3.3. Institutional costs

The difficulty of managing interests due to the vectorized **national institutional arrangement**, reaching internal **consensus**, is certainly one of the major obstacles encountered by the government when deciding to adopt a humanitarian public policy. The rules (formal and informal) that govern the **bureaucratic procedures** in the bowels of the State, as well as the ways to reach agreement, constitute the so-called institutions.[48] Either the governor knows how to reach this consensus among the agencies using the rules put in place, or, judging such costs to be too high, he avoids measures that require such skills. It takes skill to navigate this **structural organization**.

Therefore, it must be stressed that such costs are not limited to the laws limitations that are already in place in a given country, as these are already valued in the decision's legal costs. In fact, the institutional costs are linked to the procedures related to the search for internal consensus, which demands from the government a great articulation prior to the decision-making process and the execution of such a policy.

Taking Brazil, for example, the Bill 153/2020, which regulates the legal effects of the Commission and the Inter-American Court of Human Rights' decisions in Brazil, is being processed in the Chamber of Deputies. This project is restricted to guaranteeing immediate enforceability to the indemnities fixed by the two international organizations[49], leaving aside the implementation of other kind' measures. Regardless this limitation, such a legislative project is interesting because it **tries to reduce the intrinsic (institutional) costs to execute the Commission's decisions internally.**

Consensus is expensive.[50] In some explanations provided by the States themselves to the Commission, in order to justify the noncompliance with one or another measure, these difficulties in negotiations between the State Powers stand out, mainly due to the formal and informal rules put in place (such as the Powers' separation).[51]

Knowing the internal institutional arrangements 'bureaucratic idiosyncrasies is the government's task, who needs to have a thorough knowledge of these rules. Eventual disrepute or lack of knowledge about the **intrinsic limits to public administration** by the Executive Branch can lead the government to sign an agreement in face of something that **it is not even able to implement.**

This hypothesis can be corroborated by the fact that, even in friendly solutions, there is a high rate of non-compliance with measures. Choosing tools poorly is not something that only the Commission is subjected to. The governor needs to know that the measures implementation, due to the rules put in place, can be made impossible by other bodies and Powers' resistance, which can hinder the implementation process.

It is true that the country's internal rules can make the solutions' political-administrative process proposed by the Commission extremely difficult. Furthermore, these barriers can be enhanced by the abusive use (by some opposing political and legal actors) of procedural maneuvers (such as petitions and administrative and judicial resources) aimed at creating barriers for the agent.

> Crucial norm for the survival of democracy is what we call the **institutional reserve**. Reserve means "patient self-control, restraint and tolerance" or "the action to limit the use of a legal right". (...) It can be understood as the act of avoiding actions that, although they respect the law's letter, clearly violate its spirit.[52]

It is worrying that this institutional costs' weighing up may be taking place only after the agreements' signing at the IACHR, making this problem worse. There may even be the government's willingness to comply, but the execution does not occur due to the politician's lack of capacity to function as an articulator of the implementation, or even to promote changes in the corporate arrangements that prevent them (acting as a true **institutional entrepreneur**).[53]

Another relevant factor is the continuous alternation of Power, with legislatures and agents succeeding each other throughout some IACHR solutions' deferred fulfillment. This alternation causes agreements between organs and powers to undergo substantive changes due to successive elections 'possible results. The political ability to promote the consensus' continuity can be a factor that highlights the importance of the *political entrepreneur* figure in this context.

In short, the difficulty in carrying out internal political arrangements does not seem to be mere rhetoric by the government. Such institutional costs can outweigh the payment of a hefty compensation to a victim, a conclusion corroborated by the compliance rates with the measures. Undeniable that the Legislative and Judiciary can create obstacles (legitimate or not) to the Executive Power in the realization of certain public policies. It is the ruler who will need to be sufficiently skilled to lead them to internal consensus.

3.4. Legal costs

There are public policy tools - provided for in the IACHR's case solutions - that come up against **legal provisions** in the countries' own legal system. Trying to break with such paradigms brings a high strain on the government.

It is worth noting that, although a country's legal rules are also institutions (and therefore can be qualified as institutional courses), for didactic reasons they must be treated in their own category, as legal costs. Anyway, all these costs are intertwined, even if an analytical segmentation is done.

The lack of compatibility between the Commission's solutions with the legal paradigms and with a country's the legal tradition can be hindered, even in the principle of **the most favorable rule.**

> In the event of a possible conflict between international human rights law and domestic law, the criterion of the most favorable rule for the victim's prevalence is adopted. In other words, primacy is the norm that best projects, in each house, the human person's rights. In this regard, the art. 29 of the American Convention on Human Rights, which, in establishing interpretative rules, states that "no provision of the Convention may be interpreted to limit the enjoyment and exercise of any right or freedom that may be recognized under the laws of any of the States-parts or by Conventions' virtue to which one of those States is a party". Thus, the most favorable rule principle is enshrined, be it International Law or Internal Law.[54]

After all, the country itself may decide that a specific tool, suitable for the claimant's individual protection in the IACHR, calls into question the other protected by domestic law citizens' guarantees. For example, loosening the penal prescription may be adequate to reopen the investigation in a specific case, but it would allow the State to postpone criminal prosecution too much due to an even greater group of people.

Furthermore, the legal cost must not to be confused with the dialogues between organizations and powers necessary to create a new law, nor to change or suppress it; these costs are considered to be institutional. A bias is that of the consensus to create or to suppress a legal system's law, following the proper rules for that. Another point is the break with legal traditions and the pillars of a legal system already organized internally through legislative innovation.

When talking about legal costs, the focus should be on the **enforcing a law** costs, or even **breaking with a legal norm** or custom already ingrained in a given state, putting in the spotlight the congruence of that state's own legal system.

There are certain tools that bring legal costs that, presumably, can influence the government's **decision-making power**. For example, a public policy that brings the determination to modify a country's Military Justice's competence, sending facts practiced by military personnel to be investigated and prosecuted by the Common Justice.[55] Or the command to abolish the death penalty [56], switching it to another less severe sanction. These examples have the potential to cause an upheaval in a given country's domestic legal system, which is why they bring with them undeniable legal costs for the government to implement them.

It must be remembered that, ultimately, a society's fundamental ideas support the laws that govern its relations. Therefore, it is important to realize that the violation of these legal paradigms finds resistance in the very nation's underlying ideas. This approach is important because it highlights the ideas' important role in case of eventual institutions' historical permanence or changes.

Of course, ideas are not immutable, but certainly changing them requires a lot of effort on the social group part.

> The turn towards ideas has been a useful corrective to the new institutionalism's approaches' limits and a tacit recognition of its difficulties in explaining change. (...) The turn to-

<blockquote>
wards ideas undermines the new older institutionalisms' basic premise, that is, that institutions are in stable balance, with fixed rationalist preferences (rational choice institutionalism), self-reinforcing historical trajectories (historical institutionalism), or absolute cultural norms (sociological institutionalism).[57]
</blockquote>

For example, Latin American legal culture is traditionally based on the emphasis given to the Constitution and law interpretations based on legal dogma, with more emphasis on the internal angle than the external one. Still, our legal traditions are institutions that are difficult to change, as they are rooted in a strong ideological component.

<blockquote>
Latin American legal culture has adopted a legal paradigm based on three essential characteristics: a) - the pyramid with the Constitution at the legal order's apex r; (...) B) - a purified right's hermetism, with emphasis on the legal order's internal angle and the strictly normative dimension (through a legal dogmatism to remove "impure" elements from the Law); and c) - the State approach (State centered perspective), under a prism that embraces as structural and fundamental concepts the State's sovereignty in the external scope and the national security in the internal scope.[58]
</blockquote>

Therefore, it is not an easy task to transform a society's belief that international commandments have greater dignity than domestic norms.

As already mentioned, there are certain public policy tools that strive for fundamental rights' removal embedded in the countries' domestic legal orders on the grounds that they are protecting human rights. It is the case of measures that **ignore institutes conferred in the Constitutions**, such as the prescription, amnesty and immutability of res judicata.

In short, the **prescription** is a citizen's constitutional guarantee that the State has no right to sue and try to punish him forever for a criminal offense. The **amnesty** relates to an act of state forgiveness granted to crime's perpetrators, through a discretionary act, failing to apply the a criminal conviction's effects. Ultimately, the **res judicata** is the final decision on a case, and it is not normally possible to reopen it. Breaking with such institutes is a very high legal cost option for the government, because it puts his country's legal system's security at risk, as well as violates rules based on the internal legal system.

The discussion about the possibility of the Amnesty Law granted by a country to be dismissed due to its **confrontation with the international decision** content can be evidenced Claim of Non-compliance with Fundamental Precept 153. In the specific case, the Supreme Federal Court decided that the referred constitutional action was unfounded, validating , then, the Amnesty Law prepared by the Brazilian Legislative, which pardoned crimes committed at the Brazilian military regime. This seal by the Brazilian Judiciary's highest body is confronted by the decisions of the Inter-American Court of Human Rights.

In addition, high legal costs are assumed when the public policy tool is **to carry out investigative acts**, especially when they concern crimes that have occurred for a long time. When the IACHR or the parties themselves propose (and accept) investigative measures (A.5) in the solutions 'design, even though it is known that the facts occurred decades ago, it is assumed that they already know the strong chances that such measures will not bring really effective results. Remember that convicting someone with fragile elements about his guilt - in view of the Commission's investigative mandate - would be a mistake as big as those made in the previous humanitarian violation (from which the duty to investigate arose).

In fact, investigating is not just any task and the time passage worsens the chances of success. Furthermore, there are **rules that limit the investigation**, such as judicial measures to close investigations; and the investigative tools are not always available and able to reach such old facts, such as the time for keeping computer information (term of 1 year, according to art. 13 of the Marco Civil da Internet - Law 12.965 / 14). If other remedial tools exist, perhaps the investigative tool should be used only when it is feasible to deliver concrete results on the violators' fault.

Hence, when the IACHR endorses the measure's provision

such as this in the design of a case solution, it may be increasing this measure's implementation costs too much, since the government will hardly be able to overcome the existing legal obstacles without having to, to do so, violate humanitarian precepts crystallized in your own country legal orbit.

3.5. Political costs

The government officials' expected utility calculation before implementing a certain public policy is added to their prediction of **impact on the electorate**, with the difficulty of determining what are the measures that should actually be carried out from their voters' point of view, as the people tend to be interested in varied and not always coincident objects.

This requires that the government does not seek to meet a limited social group's restricted desires, since it is necessary, knowing these multiple existing interests, to make many sectors of society see themselves contemplated with public policies that appeal to them.

> In the real world, people's preference ratings are not identical (...). The government must execute a complex combination of many policies, some pleasing a majority, some pleasing the other majority and some pleasing only a minority with intense feelings about relation to them.[59]

As already mentioned, **broader magnitude and scope public policies are more likely to not generate resistance and electoral capital loss**.

There is also the possibility for the government official to take into account the risks of political support loss due to obstacles that, even though they do not directly affect their voters, are apt to be linked to their ethical-political image. Although this political cost goes far beyond the violation victim's vote, it can generate the awareness of those who share the idea that the government's non-performance stance is inadequate.

For example, the analysis of the IACHR's case follow-up report reveals that some of the violations pointed out did not even refer to the country's natives, but the ruler ended up implementing measures in favor of these foreigners. In this case, **linking the political image to good actions involving situations that generate social empathy can be a factor that encourages compliance with the measures**.

A good example may be the case [60] which deals with the risk of deporting a Jamaican citizen to his origin country, who was in the United States to seek treatment for a serious infectious disease. The victim had not been deported until that moment. This fact needs to be highlighted, since, as it is known that the United States does not boast good statistics on compliance with measures recommended by the IACHR, it still seems to have analyzed the risks of political wear and tear. By partially complying with designs like these, even though it was known that there would be no violation victims' vote loss (who is a foreigner), the government official demonstrates that he does not necessarily count votes per head, but may be conducting by groups by ideologies or partisanship.

CHAPTER 4. FACTORS INFLUENCING THE IACHR'S SOLUTIONS' IMPLEMENTATION

4.1. Political regimes' freedom degree

Common sense already indicates that freer countries are more likely to seek more efficient means and mechanisms to protect the rights and guarantees of their citizens, even if they come from exogenous interventions. Remember here the important role of ideas in the internal paradigms crystallization or change process (as advocated by ideational institutionalism).

Investigating the **political regimes' freedom** degree question qualifies as essential, as it can confirm or **demystify** the idea that freer countries are good adherents to the IACHR's solutions.

It is important to note that the presumed intrinsic costs of such a variable are multiple, ranging from the budgetary choice to institutional costs aspect, legal and political. Therefore, the theme deserves different treatment. The the political regime's freedom degree was chosen as an **approximate variable (proxy)** to try to highlight the political, institutional and legal costs faced by the government when deciding whether or not to comply with a case solution from the Commission.

In spite of the fact that some free countries have not opted to formally adhere to the System, the country's freedom degree can facilitate the social acceptance of eventual international interference, as long as they are seen as favorable to the democratic pillars' strengthening.

There is no denying that the attempt to demonstrate the relations involving the political regime's freedom degree with the solutions' fulfillment is not so simple. The main obstacle lies in categorizing a regime as **free**, **partially free** or **not free**. Such terminologies are really open.

Due to this conceptual inaccuracy, it's best to use *Freedom House's* annual report [61], which takes into account the protective framework of citizens' freedoms (vectors about respect for political rights and civil liberties).

In this classification, the **concrete capacity for the implementation of political and civil rights** by States was taken into account, and not only the guarantees provided for in the domestic legislation's abstract. Therefore, the fact that a free country does not adhere to the regional system is not so relevant here.

This proxy variable seems important because it ends up summarizing a certain community's traditions and customs, showing (by approximation) the costs to break them due to the need of internalizing the IACHR's solutions.

Countries with a **higher freedom degree have less resistance to implement humanitarian public policies**, and, on the contrary, the failure to carry out actions in this humanitarian path can be decisive for the loss of domestic political support. In any case, it must be said that there were two ways of measuring a regime's freedom degree. The first concerns the **nominal classification** given to the freedom degree (free, partially free and not free). The second concerns the freedoms score, as advocated by Freedom House. It is decided here to use the nominal category, as it guarantees a certain homogeneity.

Chart 2 – Political regime's freedom degree[62]

Country	Political rights	Civil liberties	Freedom Rate	Freedoms score	Classification
Argentina	2	2	2	79	Free
Bahamas	1	1	1	92	Free
Belize	1	2	1.5	87	Free
Bolivia	3	3	3	68	Partially
Brazil	2	2	2	81	Free
Canada	1	1	1	99	Free
Chile	1	1	1	95	Free
Colombia	3	4	3.5	63	Partially
Cuba	7	6	6.5	15	Not free
El salvador	2	3	2.5	69	Free
Ecuador	3	3	3	59	Partially
United States of America	1	1	1	90	Free
Grenada	1	2	1.5	89	Free
Guatemala	4	4	4	54	Partially
Guyana	2	3	2.5	74	Free
Haiti	5	5	5	41	Partially
Honduras	4	4	4	45	Partially
Jamaica	2	3	2.5	75	Free
Mexico	3	3	3	65	Partially
Nicaragua	4	3	3.5	54	Partially
Paraguay	3	3	3	64	Partially
Peru	2	3	2.5	71	Free
Dominican Republic	3	3	3	70	Partially
Trinidad and Tobago	2	2	2	81	Free
Uruguay	1	1	1	98	Free
Venezuela	5	5	5	35	Partially

This informations are of the utmost importance because, since countries are classified as **free** and **not so free** (these encompassing[63] the *partially free* e *not free*), it is possible to test these variables' influence (positive or negative) on the solutions' total compliance rates.

With the information crossing, it appears that, as the cases are linked to **not so free** regimes, the chances that such solutions raise the **partially fulfilled** or **totally not fulfilled** status increase. Cases linked to countries with **freer** bias, on the other hand, would be more likely to take a more active position in face of the solutions **fulfillment**, since this humanistic guise is consistent with these societies institutional and ideological pillars.[64]

4.2. State Form

One of the most intriguing points about the public policies originating from the Commission implementation concerns the hypothesis that there is a **relationship between the State form and the respective propensity for the total *designs* execution.**

As we have said about the political regime's freedom degree, the costs intrinsic to this variable are multiple, ranging from the budgetary choice to legal, institutional and political aspect. Again, a ***proxy* variable** is used to try to expose political, legal, economic and institutional barriers to the execution of such measures.

> One of the most significant political system's aspects to affect public policy is whether it is federal or unitary. In unitary systems, the existence of a clear chain of command, or hierarchy, linking the different government levels to each other, in a superior / subordinate relationship, reduces the of multilevel governance and policy-making complexity.[65]

The intention is to ascertain whether cases linked to **unitary countries** are more likely to fully comply with the solution designs, since lower costs are assumed for processing internalization procedures.

It is possible to see that **unitary countries tend to be smaller and, therefore, have a more limited Gross Domestic**

Product (or GDP)[66]. Even so, they are also expected to have simpler rules for processing procedures, since there is no marked competences and attributions distribution among numerous autonomous internal units. They work from the few legislative bodies and less autonomous local executives 'perspective. Therefore, the institutional costs of such places appear to be lower than that of federated countries.

In the chart below, it is possible to see the **clear relationship between GDPs, population size and the way they are configured internally (federal or unitary)**. It is noticed that, as a rule, larger countries have higher GDPs and are organized through Federation.

Chart 3 – State form, GDP, country size and population [67]

Country	State form	Country size (km²)	GDP (dollars)	Population
United States of America	Federation	9.831.510	7.946.996.000.000	321.418.820
Brazil	Federation	8.515.770	1.774.724.818.900	207.847.000
Canada	Federation	9.984.670	1.550.536.520.141	35.851.774
Mexico	Federation	1.964.380	1.144.331.343.172	127.017.224
Argentina	Federation	2.780.400	583.168.571.071	43.416.000
Venezuela	Federation	912.050	371.336.634.589	31.108.000
Colombia	Unitary	1.141.749	292.080.155.633	48.228.000
Chile	Unitary	756.096	240.215.707.927	17.948.000
Peru	Unitary	1.285.220	192.083.721.355	31.376.000
Ecuador	Unitary	256.370	100.871.770.000	16.144.000
Cuba	Unitary	109.880	77.149.700.000	11.389.562
Dominican Rep.	Unitary	48.670	67.103.263.863	10.528.391
Guatemala	Unitary	108.890	63.794.348.774	16.342.897
Uruguay	Unitary	176.220	53.442.697.567	3.431.000
Bolivia	Unitary	1.098.580	33.196.819.571	10.724.000
Trinidad and Tobago	Unitary	5.130	27.805.745.960	1.360.088
Paraguay	Unitary	406.752	27.090.000.000	6.854.536
El Salvador	Unitary	21.040	25.850.200.000	6.126.583
Honduras	Unitary	112.490	20.152.043.003	8.075.060
Jamaica	Unitary	10.990	14.005.654.599	2.725.941
Nicaragua	Unitary	130.370	12.692.562.187	6.082.032
Bahamas	Federation	13.880	8.884.441.432	388.019
Haiti	Unitary	27.750	8.877.465.911	10.711.067
Guyana	Unitary	214.970	3.166.029.055	767.085
Belize	Federation	22.970	1.763.000.000	359.287
Grenada	Unitary	340	978.148.148	106.825

Despite the relationships shown above, **it cannot be said** that larger, federated countries with higher GDP are more likely to fully comply with case solutions. Especially because bigger countries have more wealth, but they also spend more to maintain the federations' intrinsic structures.

As stated, countries that have a streamlined administrative structure (because they are territorially larger, especially the federated ones) and, therefore, **large corporations and Powers have even more difficulty in reaching the consensus necessary to give concrete form to very complex public policies.** As much as the budget is, as a rule, larger than that of a unitary country, institutional, political and legal costs can weigh more to achieve the joint efforts.

> In federal countries, governments find it difficult to develop consistent and coherent policies, as national policies, in most areas, require intergovernmental agreement, involving complex, extensive and time-consuming negotiations that are not always successful.[68]

Furthermore, unitary countries, being less economically self-sufficient, can do more to maintain a greater humanitarian label when demanded in the outer orbit.[69]

Federated countries are less likely to fully comply with case solutions within the IACHR's scope. This certainly reinforces the institutional costs' influence on the government officials' decision to not fully comply with the designs. Conversely, money does not appear as a central element. Anyway, this conclusion is relevant because it reinforces the thesis that trying to **homogenize** the **solution** designs (applying the same formula for unitary and federated countries) can weaken their fulfillment.

CHAPTER 5. HUMAN RIGHTS IMPLEMENTATION: COMPLIANCE WITH IACHR CASES

5.1. Documentation and information

The Inter-American Commission on Human Rights recognizes the importance of monitoring solutions as a means of effectivating human rights:

> Throughout its trajectory, the Commission has consolidated the practice of monitoring its reports through the preparation of specific monitoring reports, which aim to assess compliance with recommendations previously issued. The Commission demonstrated that assessing the effectiveness and efficacy of both the recommendations made by the IACHR to the States, through the petitions and cases system, as the follow-up, is an essential aspect to which each organization must redouble its efforts.[70]

For this reason, the Commission publishes its case follow-up report every year. The year report is, therefore, nothing more than an update (considering the previous years history) on the cases' progress and, mainly, on the States' position in relation to the recommendations or agreements reached in the Commission over the course of decades. This indicates that the analysis of a single report is sufficient for the work, and it is not necessary to make a cross-reference to all the others that preceded it.

The IACH's follow-up report published in 2017[71] reports the cases that have been processed (in a non-confidential manner) in the previous 15 years and concerning the countries linked to the Organization of American States, whether those that have already been definitively resolved or those that are still being processed by the Commission.

It must be emphasized that not all the cases that were processed in the IACHR were mentioned in the follow-up report. There are other cases that went through in secrecy, for example. Information on these classified cases will only be accessible in the IACHR's report after the State's recalcitrance to provide the solution indicated in a confidential report sent to the country. This is the rite established in articles 50 and 51 of the American Convention on Human Rights. However, the 207 cases mentioned in the IACHR follow-up report published in 2017 are already a sufficient sample..

The case follow-up report does not always contain all the necessary information, leaving **gaps**. Partial **omission** was seen in the document when it mentioned the case but did not provide all the data. For example, with regard to friendly settlements fully complied with, there is no mention in the IACHR's report as to what measures were agreed and, therefore, implemented. Hence, only with the Commission's approval agreement submission petition analysis it was possible to discover what were the measures provided for in the drawing.

Still regarding the informational gaps in the report, a complete data omission was detected. There was a lack of zeal in making the follow-up report, as was the case with Petition 279/2003, whose compliance *status* was not shown in the chart.

In addition, there was an **inaccuracy** in categorizing some case solutions as fully met, partially met, or even unfulfilled. There is even a case in which it seemed appropriate to categorize the status as partially fulfilled, but it was considered by the IACHR to be pending compliance. An example is that in all cases in Jamaica there is a similar response and action on the part of the aforementioned State, in most cases being categorized as partially fulfilled (Cases 12.069, 12.183, 11.826, 11.843, 11.846, 11.847, 12.275, 12,347, 12,418 and 12,447). In Case 12.417, also from Jamaica, the Commission chose to categorize it as pending compliance, without having sufficient reasons to do so, since the factual situation is similar to the other cases.

Another example of this type of failure is in Case 12.632 of Argentina, in which there is apparent compliance with the advertising measure and, even so, the case status is given as pending compliance.

Finally, the information in the report was not always sufficient to determine which tools were complied with or unfulfilled by the violating States..

Failures in no way affect the **advances' recognition.** After 2017,[72] there was an undeniable structural evolution in the Commission's case follow-up report, especially with regard to greater clarity in the mention of the measures specifically provided for in the solution drawings, as well as which of these had already been effectively complied with. Likewise, other advances could be seen.

For example, an essential issue was corrected about the lack of consideration given the advanced compliance state with the tools. In this case, the tools did not receive a different categorization in their fulfillment status, as they did not reach their complete closure, even if the progress towards its complete implementation was clear.

Therefore, although there has been a more adequate gradation due to the partial tools fulfillment (partially fulfilled and those with substantial partial fulfillment[73]), in its 2019 report, the IACHR maintained the same disproportionate concepts of partial compliance with the solution (as a whole), matching designs in which only one measure has been complied with with designs in which only one measure remains to be implemented[74]; of one sort or another, all are still **considered only partially fulfilled.**

Another novelty was that the Commission became concerned with the **type of impact (structural or individual)** that each of the measures may have in the violating country's humanitarian context. That is, if the tool acts in favor of a satisfactory individual intervention or if it structurally modifies the reality put in that violating country. This is an advance, but the IACHR could have evolved in the sense of also considering the measures 'impact (and their respective presumed costs) with respect to the government that must comply with it, going on to justify the reason for its case-by-case need and, mainly about its suitability for that particular contextual reality.

Even when such gaps were still present, the IACHR's report (and related documentation), published in 2017, **already allowed the extraction of relevant information.** The data sought were: **type of solution** adopted for each case (friendly or meritorious), **cases' status** (fully met, partially met or not met), the **numerical measures' complexity**[75] contained in the solution design, **types of measures** used in the construction of each of the public policy designs and, finally, which of these measures were **complied with or not complied with** by the State.

It was through the case follow-up report's detailed analysis that the existence of standard tools used in the composition of each of the 207 public policy designs listed in the document was revealed..

This classification in tools was possible because the solutions usually bring the same measures, which indicates the **existence of possible historical patterns in the solutions' design.** There was, therefore, the observation and construction of ideal types, making it possible to fit these various generic tool concepts with what is found concretely in the follow-up report..

Based on this cataloging work, 7 *nodality* tools, 9 *authority* tools, 9 *treasure* tools categories, 3 *organization* tools categories were detected, as well as 1 *non-repetition of similar violations generic* measure.[76]

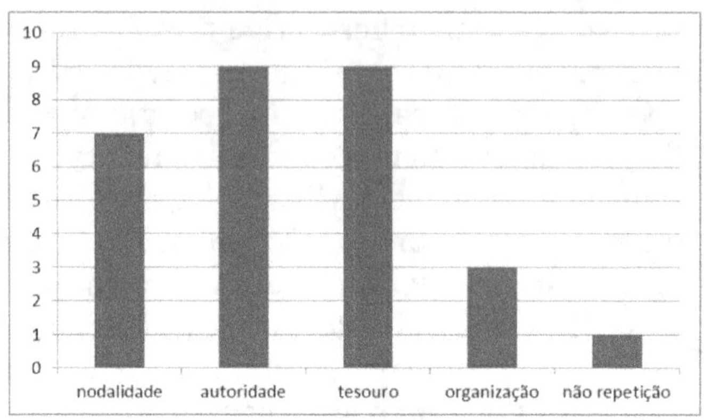

These tools categories used are inspired by the classifica-tion contained in the NATO model.[77] Summing up, the afore-mentioned model advocates that there are four major groups of tools that can be used in the public policy design: **informa-tion** (*nodality* tools), command **power** (*authority* tools), **money** (treasure *tools*) and bodies and institutions' possible **structural modification** (*organizational* tools).

The tools were readjusted and divided into similar types, adding one more tool, namely, the non-repetition of violations generic measure.

Therefore, it became possible to clarify some points: friendly solutions prevail over meritorious ones, and which of these are more likely to fully comply; the solution' numerical complexity pattern in each case and their propensity to fully comply with the design; the compliance rate with each of these tools in isolation, analyzed based on the number of times they appear in the follow-up report, which would provide the for-mulation of an overall effectiveness rate for each tool; and, finally, cross-check information as a form of state and political regime's freedom degree due to the complexity of the solution designs and, mainly, ascertain the greater or lesser propensity to fully comply with the design.

5.2. Fulfillment *status*

It was found that, among the **207 cases** provided for in the IACHR's follow-up report, 48 have the fully fulfilled status, 126 the partially fulfilled status and 33 the totally unfulfilled status (pending fulfillment).

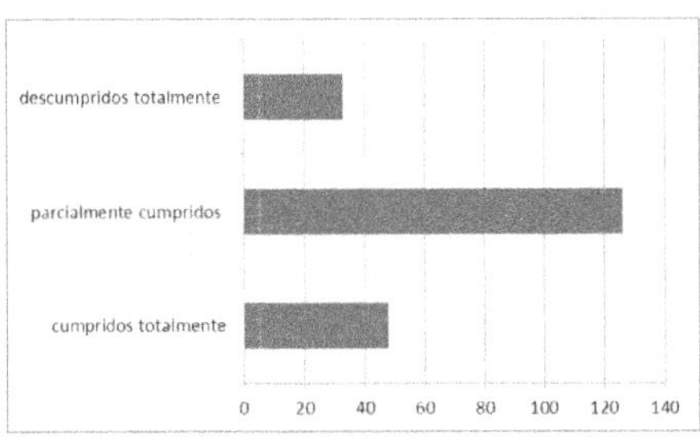

A States with the most cases mentioned in the IACHR's follow-up report, the respective State form, as well as these cases' status analysis was carried out (in descending order), country by country.

Chart 4 – State form and IACHR cases fulfillment status[78]

Legend:
FFDFS - fully fulfilled due to friendly settlement.
FFDMD - fully fulfilled due to merit decision.
PFFS - partially fulfilled by friendly settlement.
PFMD - partially fulfilled by merit decision.
PAFFS - pending arising from a friendly settlement.
PAFMS - pending arising from merit solution.

Country	State form	FFDFS	FFDMD	PFFS	PFMD	PAFFS	PAFMS
Ecuador	Unitary	1	0	27	3	0	0
United States of America	Federation	0	1	0	10	0	14
Argentina	Federation	8	0	10	2	1	1
Guatemala	Unitary	1	0	9	7	0	0
Mexico	Federation	6	1	4	2	0	2
Peru	Unitary	5	1	5	3	0	0
Colombia	Unitary	2	2	6	4	0	0
Brazil	Federation	1	0	1	10	0	1
Chile	Unitary	7	1	1	3	0	0
Jamaica	Unitary	0	0	0	7	0	1
Paraguay	Unitary	1	1	1	2	0	0
Bolivia	Unitary	4	0	1	0	0	0
Bahamas	Federation	0	0	0	2	0	2
Venezuela	Federation	0	0	2	0	1	0
Uruguay	Unitary	1	1	0	1	0	0
Grenada	Unitary	0	0	0	3	0	0
Cuba	Unitary	0	0	0	1	0	1
Guyana	Unitary	0	0	0	1	0	1
Honduras	Unitary	2	0	0	0	0	0
Belize	Federation	0	0	0	0	0	1
Trinidad and Tobago	Unitary	0	0	0	0	0	1
Haiti	Unitary	0	0	0	0	0	1
Canada	Federation	0	0	0	1	0	0
Dominican Rep.	Unitary	1	0	0	0	0	0
El salvador	Unitary	0	0	0	1	0	0
Nicaragua	Unitary	0	0	0	1	0	0

To better understand the data presented in the chart, it is necessary to have knowledge about some of these **case solutions' status' concepts.** The IACHR itself is the one who points out in the case follow-up report which are the parameters for the decision to be qualified as fully complied with, partially complied with or pending compliance (not complied with until then).

Total compliance: these are the cases in which the State has fully complied with all the recommendations published by

Despite these objective concepts' existence, there are problems caused by the wide **status' conceptual scope,** especially in face of **partially fulfilled solutions**. This is because the solutions can be categorized as partially fulfilled due to the fact that only one of the tools has been defaulted (even if all the others provided for in the drawing have been complied with) or even when the country has partially fulfilled only one of them and totally failed the rest.

It is possible that this conceptual equalization has the power to drive government officials towards the **option of complying with only one of the measures, as the partial compliance status is still achieved.** After all, the ruler always acts as strategically as possible, and aiming for the best alternative available concretely in the condition he finds himself in.

Considering that the costs of fully complying with the solution can be high, the decision maker would satisfy part of the collective desire to see the IACHR's humanist determinations met. It is not denied that this is one of the potential explanations for the decisions partially complied with prevalence when compared with decisions fully complied with or totally not complied with (pending compliance).

In order to correct such terminological distortion, it is appropriate for the Commission to create a **compliance gradual**

scale (according to the number of tools foreseen in the design and the total number of measures completed) so as to stimulate the increasing compliance with the recommendation or agreement..

In this context, imagine an IACHR recommendation that includes five tools in its design, only one of which has been fully complied with, and the other four are pending compliance (not complied with). The relationship that should be included, regarding the compliance status with the measure, is expressed in the fraction 1/5 or 20%. Otherwise, using the same tags, in which four tools have been complied with, and only one of them is pending compliance, the existing ratio would be expressed in the fraction 4/5 or 80%. Certainly, this criterion could help to stimulate the government's efforts to fulfill the solutions coming from the IACHR.

5.3. Forms of solutions (meritorious and friendly)

There are two ordinary ways of solving a case presented to the Commission: the **friendly** and the **meritorious** way (recommendation imposed unilaterally by the IACHR to the State). The first form is initiated in the procedure provided for in the American Convention on Human Rights 'Article 49, while the second is based on the provisions of the same normative diploma's Article 51.

Compulating the follow-up report published in 2017, it is possible to notice that of the 207 cases listed, 109 are linked to the friendly settlement, with 98 being related to the meritorious way.

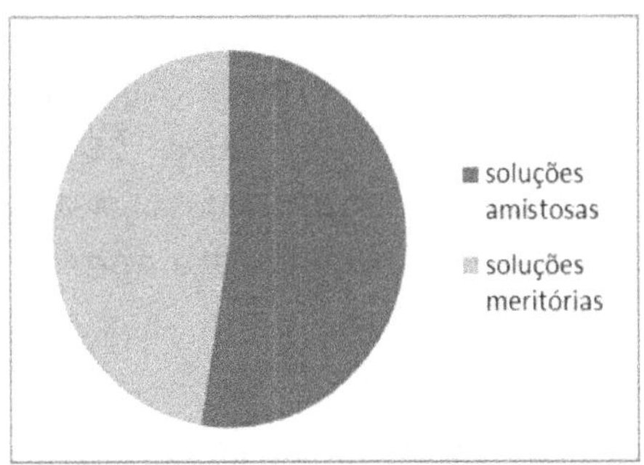

Of the **fully complied** cases, **40 are friendly** and **8 are meritorious.** Among those **partially fulfilled, 67 are friendly and 59 are meritorious.** Finally, in **non-fulfilled cases (pending compliance),** only **2 are friendly and 31 are meritorious.**

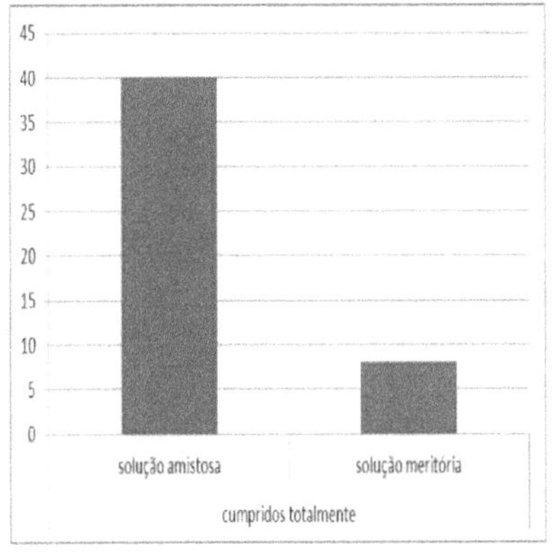

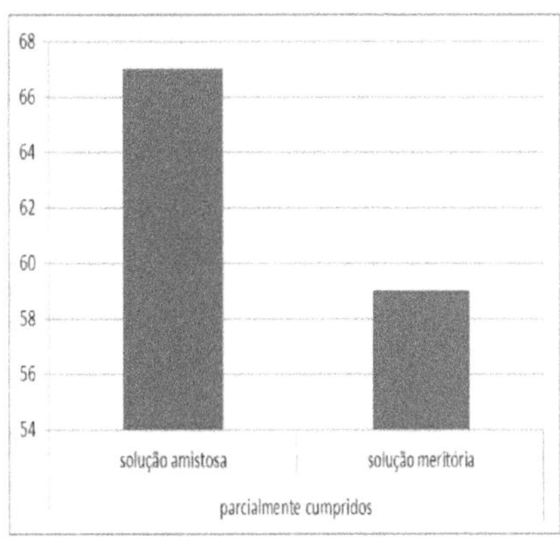

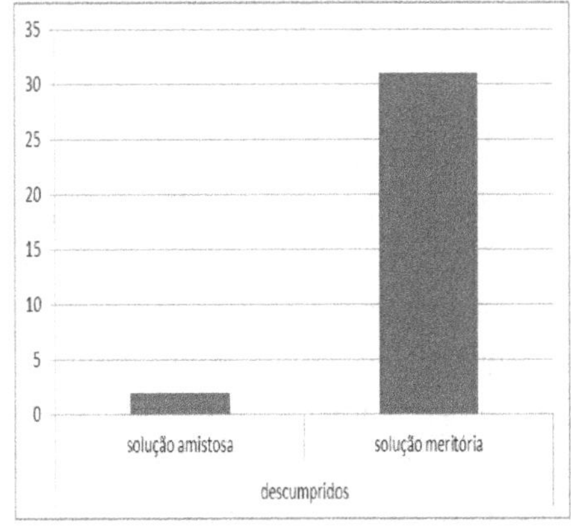

Both **friendly** and **meritorious** solutions **tend to partial compliance**. In relation to other cases, however, friendly solutions generate more total compliance than non-compliance, while meritorious solutions generate more non-compliance than full compliance.

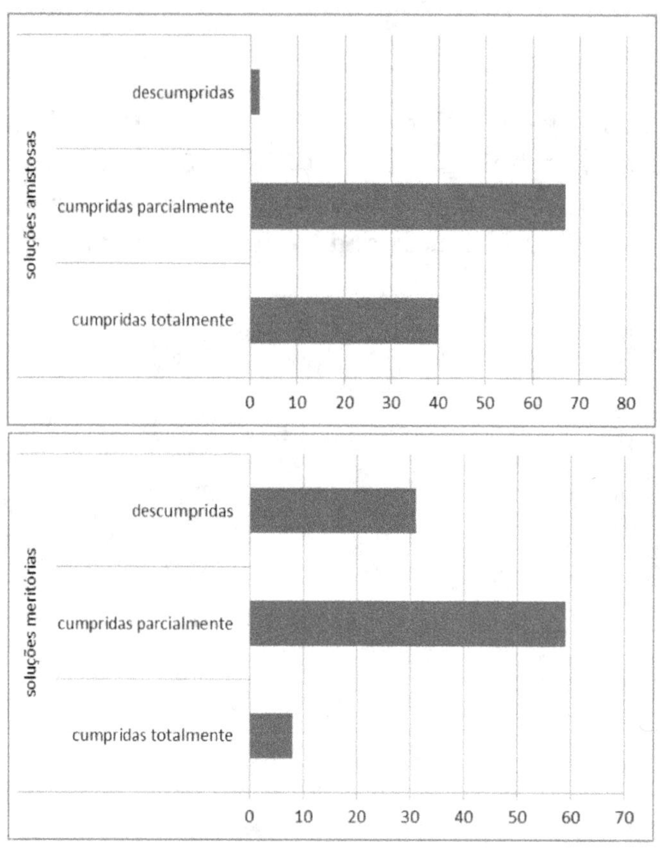

It can be noted from this information that the greatest propensity to **comply** with cases is **friendly**. In this scenario, solutions are agreed between the parties involved (government and victim) at the beginning of the legal procedure and, afterwards, submitted for approval. This formatting ensures greater adaptation to the government's realities (at least hypothetically), as well as meeting the petitioners' reparative wishes. With the caveat that ill-informed government officials (and who fail to realize the real implementation costs) can enter into unenforceable agreements.

On the other hand, since an initial friendly solution was not possible, we move on to the next phase: making a merit or background solution. In this case, **the IACHR unilaterally decides the public policy that must be implemented by the violating State.** The Commission designs the solution, using the tools as it sees fit, and forwards them to compliance. The petitioner is not open to introducing measures to repair his suffering in the recommendations; the only possibility that remains is to sign a friendly settlement in the course of the merit settlement procedure already set in motion. If there is no agreement, the design will be unilaterally determined by the IACHR, and the government can only comply with it as recommended.

Another interesting possibility was seen in the cases follow-up report: that of meritorious remedies already established and, in the course of the procedure for monitoring the execution, an agreement of wills occurs between the petitioners and the State. In these situations, the Commission usually maintains the original solution classification to the case, that is, as a meritorious one, despite the friendly settlement. As occurred in the following cases: 12,632 from Argentina, 11,725 from Chile, 12,249 from El Salvador, 9,903 from the United States, 11,625 from Guatemala, 9,111 from Guatemala, and 11,607 from Paraguay. This classification should be modified, since the subsequent consensus causes the initial impositivity typical of the meritorious solution to collapse.

In other situations, the opposite has occurred. And in these cases, despite that compliance with the demand has been initiated through an IACHR recommendation, in which there was a subsequent agreement, the Commission classified the case resolution as a friendly settlement, which seems to be better than maintaining the meritorious rating. In this sense, see Guatemala's Case 10,855.

In one way or another, it is important to emphasize that the cases that underwent such *Kafkaesque* **transmutation** did not show a considerable increase in the compliance's total rate. That's because none of the aforementioned cases had the fully complied with status in the follow-up report, which indicates that these drawings 'complexity may have been more determinant for their total non-compliance than the change in the solution form. Especially because it is possible that the negotiation range is seriously linked to the precepts already designed in the previous merit solution, which does not allow such discretion.

5.4. *Designs* and public policy tools

5.4.1. Public policies drawings

Humanitarian public policy, within the Inter-American Human Rights System's scope, is conceptualized as the sum of the government's, natural people's and organizations '(including supranational) efforts, in a specific place and time, through the rational use of specific and appropriate tools, for the resolution of an issue involving the human rights application, aiming at the victims 'reparation and the non-repetition of similar facts.

It emerges from such a concept that it is not possible to talk about solving IACHR cases without, implicitly, existing a specific public policy. In addition, there is no public humanitarian policy without the **commitment that there will be a sum of efforts by agents and internal corporations** (related to the very State's structure) **aimed at achieving this relevant humanitarian objective.** Therefore, it is essential to understand that the mere case solution, within the Commission's scope, does not lead to the real public policy implementation; it depends on the efforts that the government will put in internally as a political entrepreneur.

In any case, the first phase to achieve this goal is that there is a balanced project previously designed by the IACHR, or even by consensus between the violating country's representative and the violation victim (or whoever represents him/her), containing appropriate tools and belonging to one or more categories.

For this reason, not only in the case of friendly solutions, but also in the case of decisions on the merits, all efforts must be directed so that the design is adequate and, therefore, does not become an impediment to the humanitarian public policy realization by the Head of State or Head of Government.

The specialized literature even brings an **public policy cycle** ideal design, formed by five stages [80]: agenda setting, policy formulation (instrument and design), political decision making, policy implementation and evaluation. Of course, there is no immutable rite, since the phases of this cycle are usually intertwined and may even end up overlapping.

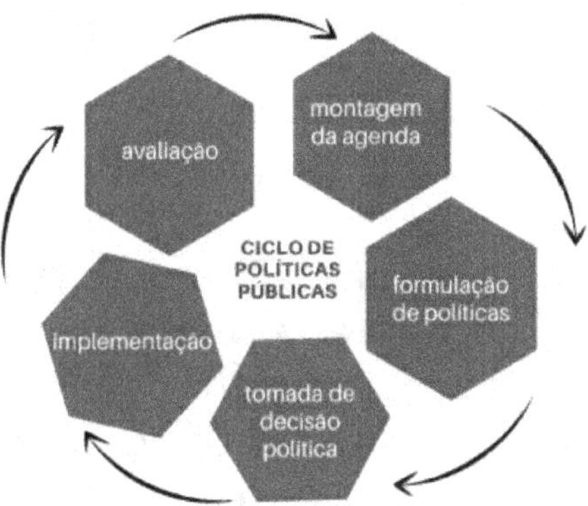

Ordinarily, a public policy should start when **the government recognizes a public problem as being also politically relevant and puts it on the agenda.** However, this is not quite the case with solutions originating from the IACHR.

In fact, the government official only acts when there is an international demand in place and, then, he finds himself compelled to formulate that solution amicably, under penalty of having an imposing public policy design formulated by the IACHR against him. In other words, **the agenda phase only appears after the dispute starts at the international level or when the case solution is already outlined (recommendation).**

Therefore, the priority sense regarding the implementation of such a public policy design is the result of exogenous pressure from the international body, which forces this issue to appear on the country's agenda, and does not allow sufficient prior deliberation at the domestic level.

It is possible to notice, then, that one of the humanitarian public policy cycle's most important phases concerns its **design** (formulation), that is, how and with what instruments this public policy will be formed. Only after it is formulated that it passes through the political agenda's sieve, which constitutes an **expected procedure inversion**.

Roughly speaking, the international public policy design formulation is similar to an executive plan or an architectural design model. It is not uncommon for the plant to come ready (mainly in meritorious decisions), making the State struggle to try to make that project come true in the real world. The problem is that there are numerous factors that count against this implementation, including resources and the need to convince partners to execute the plan.

If the drawings are already linked to certain tools, there will be little margin of discretion for internal agents to choose the least costly implementation methods. For this reason, these binding tools' study and understanding are of utmost importance in the implementing public policies context. If chosen in an untimely or unreasonable way, the entire implementation plan for a given public policy is at risk.

> These tools, (...) together, constitute the content of the toolbox from which governments must choose when building or creating public policies. Policy design elevates the analysis and practice of choosing policy instruments - specifically tools for policy implementation - to a central study focus.[81]

There are several **tools** that can be used in a public policy design, which are not provided for in an IACHR list or in a normative instrument. To fill this gap, these instruments will be grouped here in different types and ideal genres in order to facilitate the reader's understanding.

The said tools do not contain a single peculiarity, so that it is not entirely correct to restrict them to a single genre. These instrument' overriding characteristics will be taken into account, that is, whether they are predominantly economic, informational, coercive or organizational. It is interesting, therefore, that **ideal types** are used, and not perfect and exhaustive reality descriptions.

In any case, it is appropriate to know such taxonomies, as they help to demonstrate the multifaceted range of instruments types that are available when designing a public policy.

> Christopher Hood (1986a) developed a simple and powerful taxonomy, known as the "NATO model", proposing that all political tools used one of four government or control resources broad categories. He argued that governments face public problems with the use of information in their power as central political actors ("nodality"), with the use of their legal powers ("authority"), their money ("treasure") or the formal organizations at their disposal ("organization"), or NATO. Governments can use these resources to manipulate political actors, for example, withholding or making information or money available, using their coercive powers to force other actors to carry out activities that they want, or simply undertaking the activities themselves using of its own staff and expertise.[82]

Inspired by this categorization process, we began to investigate whether there was a **similar pattern** in the measures used by the Inter-American Commission on Human Rights, when making its recommendations, or even by the parties in possible friendly solutions. If this pattern were found (meeting the homogeneity criteria), it would be possible **to group these measures and start to call them truly tools.**

This cataloging work's result was surprising. The IACHR's determinations (or agreements 'measures) maintained a certain standard, which allowed its conceptualization as authentic public policy tools.

Detecting these *tools* in the IACHR's follow-up report was of utmost importance because, when it was noted that the public policies designs (friendly or meritorious) were formed by a homogeneous tools set, it was possible to measure the quantity in each design and, also, analyze their compliance rate.

5.4.2. Tools taxonomy

The IACHR's follow-up report reading, as well as the respective petition documents for the Commission violations' submission, brought up the need to categorize the measures that repeatedly appeared in the solution designs.

Such propaedeutic work showed that there is an implicit tools list that is available to the *policy designer* when building the case solution drawings. There are no express rules that oblige *players* to use these typologies in design, but in practice, they usually go for them.

The fact that the IACHR's follow-up report does not include the terminologies typical of the public policy literature may be an indication that the agents and organizations that shape these designs' view is that the measures agreed or recommended are simple obligations and duties aimed at violating countries, and not real humanitarian public policies, which would be a serious mistake.

Each of these public policy tools revolves around certain **social intervention genres**. Illustratively, there are public policy tools that use information as a contribution to carry out a necessary social change (advertising campaigns), while others use the wealth distribution for this (exemption from taxes for a given gender). Thus, in this research, public policy tools were divided based on the following social transformation genres: nodality (information), authority (state authority), treasure (wealth), organization (institutional and organizational structure) and generic measures of non-repetition . It should be underlined, as appropriate, that all the tools of the inter-American NATO model have a bias of similar violations' non-repetition.

There is no denying that the construction of an adequate **typology** to categorize public policy tools into genres is not entirely new. What this study did was to refine the existing doctrine, perfecting the model for the present context.

Neither in the NATO model, nor in the present **inter-American NATO model**, are the tools free from the interference of attributes related to other categories or genres 'instruments. For example, there is no need to talk about the obligation to build a museum in the victim's honor (a nodality tool) without realizing that this money expenditure will act as a disincentive for possible new violations (treasure tool). Therefore, **there is no pure and hermetic tools type, but a necessary interlacing between all of them**. We took into account what is preponderant in each of them to achieve the most accurate classification.

One of the difficulties is the **complication of subsuming** the measures contained in the IACHR's follow-up report to this inter-American NATO model's tools' novel list. After all, some of the points recommended or agreed (in each case) bring a construction so complex that it is difficult to know, at once, which and how many tools are needed to meet that specific point.

For example, there is a recommendation for the governor to conduct a thorough investigation of the violation; as well as a legislative change allowing this investigation. In this case, two authority tools were accounted for, namely A.5 (investigation) and A.7 (legifying measure).[83]

With or without limitations, the classifications derived from the inter-American NATO model greatly facilitated the tools 'effectiveness measurement and, consequently, allowed to evaluate which are so complex that they make the design's implementation costs difficult for the government to bear.

5.4.3. Tools quantification

The actual costs quantification and real barriers to which government officials are subject when attempting to implement each of the public policiy tools design would require each government official's interview to find out the real obstacles they faced throughout the process. For this reason, using *proxies* and genres that represent prevalent costs, a skillful construct was conceived, using a **bayesian bias** (hypothesis evaluation by maximum likelihood), to test the hypotheses raised here.

In addition, not every tool has objective costs to be measured (with the exception of tools with an economic character). Even in the case of tools that have a predominantly economic bias, the attempt to quantify would come up against the lack of clarity in the IACHR's report: either the violation victims 'precise number is missing, or there are no such repair tools 'direct beneficiaries (relatives for example). Therefore, it is not feasible to quantify the economic costs, due to quantifying and identifying the victims and beneficiaries 'difficulty.

As an example, we mention what is contained in petition 108/2000, which deals with the Segovia Massacre in Colombia. The IACHR report mentions that there are 28 family groups that have been victimized and hypothetically benefited from the remedial measures listed in the public policy design. Another good example of this inaccuracy is Guatemala's Case 11,197, which mentions that 233 indigenous families have had their interests violated and must now be remedied. The lack of clarity lies in the fact that it is not known exactly how many people each family has.

Therefore, instead of taking into account the number of **each tools' repetitions in the same given public policy design,** it was decided to take into account only the fact that such a tool is **present** in the solution design. For example, if there is a single indemnity payment (in the amount of X) or even twenty indemnities (in the amount of 20 X), there will be the related tool launch. No weight will be given to the tools, nor they will they be multiplied depending on the times that such measure will be applied concretely due to a particular solution. After all, it may be that a single indemnity corresponds to the value of twenty other smaller indemnities, and the values consideration would make it extremely complicated to weigh all the tools that have, directly or indirectly, an economic nature.

5.5. Tools and solutions compliance

In addition to investigating the existence of some standard tools used by the IACHR, it is possible to measure the effective **compliance rate** for each of them. To this end, in light of the assessment standard used by the Inter-American Commission on Human Rights, the following were considered possible status for compliance with the tools considered in isolation: (1) **complied with**, (2) **not complied with** or (3) **without compliance information**. With this classification, it is possible to assess (using each of the tools provided for in the 207 solutions contained in the IACHR's follow-up report) the *overall effectiveness rate* of each of these instruments.

The following chart lists all the cases contained in the IACHR's follow-up report, as well as the overall compliance status of these solutions, the type of solution (friendly or meritorious), the design complexity, as well as the tools' compliance status.

Chart 5 – Case status, type of solution, design complexity and tool compliance status [84]

Legend:
TC (totally complied with)
PC (partially complied with)
N (totally not complied with)

Observation 1: solutions design complexity according to the criteria indicated in chart 11.
Observation 2: all genders and the respective tools were duly detailed in charts 6, 7, 8, 9 and 10.

Country	Case	Case status	Type of solution	Desi gn	Expected and complied with tools	Expected and not complied with tools	Expected tools and no data on compliance
Argentina	11.307	TC	Friendly	1	A.6	X	X
Argentina	11.804	PC	Friendly	39	N.1/ T.2/T.4	A.5/A.7/O.1/ O.3	A.1/A.3/A.6
Argentina	12.080	PC	Friendly	13	T.4/T.5	N.6/A.7	N.1
Argentina	12.298	PC	Friendly	18	T.4/T.5	N.1 / N.4/A.1/ A.7	X
Argentina	12.159	PC	Friendly	13	T.4/T.5	N.1 / N.7	A.1
Argentina	11.732	PC	Merit	3	A.10	N.3	X
Argentina	11.758	TC	Friendly	4	N.1/N.3/N.6	X	X
Argentina	11.796	TC	Friendly	1	T.1	X	X
Argentina	12.536	PC	Friendly	19	N.2/T.1/T.4/O.2	N.6/A.5	X
Argentina	P.242/03	PC	Friendly	12	A.7	N.1/ N.5/N.6/ A.6	X
Argentina	P. 4554/02	TC	Friendly	3	A.7/T.1	X	X
Argentina	P. 2829/02	TC	Friendly	3	A.7	X	T.1
Argentina	11.708	TC	Friendly	3	A.4/T.6	X	X
Argentina	11.833	TC	Friendly	1	O.3	X	X
Argentina	12.532	PC	Friendly	44	N.1/N.2/N.5/ A.6/O.1	A.5/T.5/O.2	A.1/A.7/A.10
Argentina	12.306	PC	Friendly	5	A.6	N.6/A.7	X
Argentina	11.670	TC	Friendly	5	N.6/A.2/A.6	X	X
Argentina	12.324	PC	Merit	8	T.1	A.5	A.3/A.7
Argentina	12.182	PC	Friendly	2	X	T.4/T.5	X
Argentina	P. 21/05	N	Friendly	13	X	N.1/N.6/A.5/ T.4/T.5	X

Country	Case	Case status	Type of solution	Design	Expected and complied with tools	Expected and not complied with tools	Expected tools and no data on compliance
Argentina	P. 21/05	N	Friendly	13	X	N.1/N.6/A.5/ T.4/T.5	X
Argentina	12.710	PC	Friendly	6	A.8	N.5/T.8	X
Argentina	12.632	N	Merit	28	X	N.1/N.3/N.6/ A.4/A.6/A.7/ A.10/T.6	X
Bahamas	12.067 / 12.068/ 12.086	PC	Merit	12	X	A.6/A.7/A.8/ A.10	T.1
Bahamas	12.265	PC	Merit	12	X	A.6/A.7/A.8/ A.10	T.1
Bahamas	12.513	N	Merit	7	X	A.6/A.7/A.8/ A.10	X
Bahamas	12.231	N	Merit	17	X	A.3/A.5/A.7/ A.8/A.10	T.1
Belize	12.053	N	Merit	8	X	A.6/A.7/A.10/ T.6	X
Bolivia	12.475	PC	Friendly	4	A.1/A.6	A.7	X
Bolivia	12.516	TC	Friendly	1	A.4	X	X
Bolivia	P. 269/05	TC	Friendly	1	T.6	X	X
Bolivia	P. 788/06	TC	Friendly	3	A.9/T.6	X	X
Bolivia	12.350	TC	Friendly	2	N.1/N.4	X	X
Brazil	12051	PC	Merit	29	N.5	A.5/A.6/A.7/ A.10/O.1	N.4/T.1

Country	Case	Case status	Type of solution	Design	Expected and complied with tools	Expected and not complied with tools	Expected tools and no data on compliance
Brazil	12051	PC	Merit	29	N.5	A.5/A.6/A.7/A.10/O.1	N.4/T.1
Brazil	11.286 / 11.407/ 11.406/ 11.416/ 11.413/ 11.417/ 11.412 e 11.415.	PC	Merit	8	A.5	A.7	A.10/O.1
Brazil	11.517	PC	Merit	5	X	A.5	A.10/T.1
Brazil	10.301	PC	Merit	8	A.7	A.1/T.1	A.5
Brazil	11.289	PC	Friendly	24	X	A.5/A.6/A.7	N.7/T.1/T.9/O.3
Brazil	11.556	PC	Merit	13	X	A.5/A.6/A.7/T.1/NR	X
Brazil	11.634	PC	Merit	18	X	A.5/A.6/A.7/A.10	N.5/T.1
Brazil	12.426/ 12.427	TC	Friendly	24	N.2/N.3/N.5/A.6/T.1/T.8/O.3	X	X
Brazil	12.001	PC	Merit	34	N.3/N.7/T.1/T.8	A.5/A.7	N.5/A.6/O.1
Brazil	12.019	N	Merit	9	X	N.5/A.5/A.7/T.1	X
Brazil	12.310	PC	Merit	8	X	A.5/A.6/A.10/T.1	X
Brazil	12.440	PC	Merit	8	T.1	A.5/A.6/A.10	X
Brazil	12.308	PC	Merit	9	N.3/T.1	A.5/A.10	X
Canada	12.586	PC	Merit	17	A.7/A.10	A.1/T.1	A.3/A.6
Chile	11.771	PC	Merit	5	X	A.5/A.7	T.1
Chile	11.715	TC	Friendly	5	N.2/T.3/T.8	X	X
Chile	P. 12.046	TC	Friendly	3	N.2/T.8	X	X
Chile	P. 11.725	PC	Merit	18	N.2/N.3/T.1	A.5/A.6/A.7	X
Chile	P. 4617/02	PC	Friendly	8	X	A.6/A.10/T.8	A.7
Chile	12.142	TC	Merit	1	T.1	X	X
Chile	12.337	TC	Friendly	13	N.1/N.7/A.7/T.1/T.8	X	X

Country	Case	Case status	Type of solution	Design	Expected and complied with tools	Expected and not complied with tools	Expected tools and no data on compliance
Chile	P. 490/03	TC	Friendly	18	N.1/N.2/N.7/ A.3/A.6/T.8	X	X
Chile	12.469	PC	Merit	5	A.3/A.7	T.1	X
Chile	12.281	TC	Friendly	5	N.1/N.6/T.1	X	X
Chile	12.195	TC	Friendly	18	N.1/N.2/N.6/ A.1/T.1/T.8	X	X
Chile	12.232	TC	Friendly	2	N.1/N.6	X	X
Colombia	11.654	PC	Merit	13	T.1	A.5/A.6/A.10/ NR	X
Colombia	11.710	PC	Merit	13	T.1	A.5/A.6/A.10/ NR	X˙
Colombia	11.712	PC	Merit	13	T.1	A.5/A.6/A.10/ NR	X
Colombia	11.141	PC	Friendly	19	T.1/O.3	N.1/A.5	N.2/A.6
Colombia	10.205	TC	Friendly	3	A.3/T.1	X	X
Colombia	12.009	TC	Merit	9	N.2/N.5/A.5/T.1	X	X
Colombia	12.448	TC	Merit	3	T.1/NR	X	X
Colombia	P. 477/05	TC	Friendly	9	N.2/A.5/T.1/T.8	X	X
Colombia	P. 401-05	PC	Friendly	18	N.2/N.4/T.1/T.8	A1/A.5	X
Colombia	10.916	PC	Merit	5	X	A.5/T.1	A.10
Colombia	P. 12.376 / P. 653	PC	Friendly	12	N.3	N.4/N.5/T.1/ T.8	X
Colombia	12.756	PC	Friendly	13	N.4	T.1/T.8	N.5/A.5
Colombia	P.108/00	PC	Friendly	23	N.2/N.3/N.4/ N.5	A.5/T.1/T.8	X
Colombia	P. 577/06	PC	Friendly	9	N.2	A.5/T.1/T.8	X
Cuba	12.476	PC	Merit	13	A.8	A.6/A.7/T.1/ NR	X
Cuba	12.477	N	Merit	9	X	A.6/A.7/T.1/ NR	X
Ecuador	11.421	PC	Friendly	8	T.1/T.4	A.1/A.5	X
Ecuador	11.439	PC	Friendly	8	T.1/T.4	A.1/A.5	X
Ecuador	11.445	TC	Friendly	8	A.1/A.5/T.1/T.4	X	X

Country	Case	Case status	Type of solution	Desi gn	Expected and complied with tools	Expected and not complied with tools	Expected tools and no data on compliance
Ecuador	11.466	PC	Friendly	8	T.1/T.4	A.1/A.5	X
Ecuador	11.584	PC	Friendly	8	T.1/T.4	A.1/A.5	X
Ecuador	11.783	PC	Friendly	8	T.1/T.4	A.1/A.5	X
Ecuador	11.868	PC	Friendly	5	T.1	A.1/A.5	X
Ecuador	11.991	PC	Friendly	8	T.1/T.4	A.1/A.5	X
Ecuador	11.478	PC	Friendly	5	T.1	A.1/A.5	
Ecuador	11.512	PC	Friendly	8	T.1/T.4	A.1/A.5	X
Ecuador	11.605	PC	Friendly	8	T.1/T.4	A.1/A.5	X
Ecuador	11.779	PC	Friendly	8	T.1/T.4	A.1/A.5	X
Ecuador	11.992	PC	Mérito	5	A.7	A.5/T.1	X
Ecuador	11.441	PC	Friendly	8	T.1/T.4	A.1/A.5	X
Ecuador	11.443	PC	Friendly	8	T.1/T.4	A.1/A.5	X
Ecuador	11.450	PC	Friendly	8	T.1/T.4	A.1/A.5	X
Ecuador	11.542	PC	Friendly	8	T.1/T.4	A.1/A.5	X
Ecuador	11.574	PC	Friendly	8	T.1/T.4	A.1/A.5	X
Ecuador	11.632	PC	Friendly	8	T.1/T.4	A.1/A.5	X
Ecuador	12.007	PC	Friendly	8	T.1/T.4	A.1/A.5	X
Ecuador	11.515	PC	Friendly	8	T.1/T.4	A.1/A.5	X
Ecuador	12.188	PC	Friendly	8	T.1/T.4	A.1/A.5	X
Ecuador	12.394	PC	Friendly	8	T.1/T.4	A.1/A.5	X
Ecuador	12.205	PC	Friendly	8	T.1/T.4	A.1/A.5	X
Ecuador	12.207	PC	Friendly	8	T.1/T.4	A.1/A.5	X
Ecuador	12.238	PC	Friendly	23	T.1/T.4	N.1/N.3/A.1/ A.5/A.8	X
Ecuador	12.558	PC	Friendly	5	T.1/T.4	A.5	X
Ecuador	12.487	PC	Merit	6	N.3	A.5/T.1	X
Ecuador	12.525	PC	Merit	2	A.3	A.7	X
Ecuador	P. 533/05	PC	Friendly	5	T.1/T.4	A.5	X
Ecuador	12.631	PC	Friendly	29	N.5/A.10/T.1/ T.8	A.5/A.7/O.1/ O.3	X
El Salvador	12.249	PC	Merit	24	N.1/N.3/T.1/T.4	A.7	N.5/O.3

Country	Case	Case status	Type of solution	Design	Expected and complied with tools	Expected and not complied with tools	Expected tools and no data on compliance
United States of America	9.903	N	Merit	4	X	A.3/A.6/A.7	X
United States of America	12.243	N	Merit	8	X	A.6/A.7/A.8/ T.1	X
United States of America	11.753	PC	Merit	4	A.3	A.6/A.7	X
United States of America	12.285	TC	Merit	4	A.3/A.6/A.7	X	X
United States of America	11.140	N	Merit	4	X	A.3/A.6/A.7	X
United States of America	11.193	PC	Merit	8	X	X	A.6/A.7/ A.10/T.1
United States of America	11.204	N	Merit	4	X	A.3/ A.6/A.7	X
United States of America	11.331	PC	Merit	11	X	A.3/A.6/A.7/ A.8/A.10	X
United States of America	12.240	PC	Merit	8	X	A.6/A.7/A.10/ T.1	X
United States of America	12.412	PC	Merit	8	X	A.6/A.7/A.10/ T.1	X
United States of America	12.430	PC	Merit	7	X	A.3/A.6/A.7/ A.10	X
United States of America	12.439	PC	Merit	8	X	X	A.6/A.7/ A.10/T.1
United States of America	12.421	PC	Merit	8	X	A.6/A.7/A.10/ T.1	X
United States of America	12.534	PC	Merit	1	X	A.9	X
United States of America	12.644	N	Merit	12	X	A.3/A.6/A.7/ A.10/T.1	X

Country	Case	Case status	Type of solution	Desi gn	Expected and complied with tools	Expected and not complied with tools	Expected tools and no data on compliance
United States of America	12.562	N	Merit	11	X	A.1/A.3/A.6/ A.7/A.10	X
United States of America	12.626	PC	Merit	18	X	A.5/A.6/A.7/ A.10/T.1	N.5
United States of America	12.776	N	Merit	8	X	A.5/A.6/A.7/ T.1	X
United States of America	11.575/12. 333 e 12.341	N	Merit	12	X	A.3/A.6/A.7/ A.10/T.1	X
United States of America	12.864	N	Merit	7	X	A.3/A.6/A.7/ A.10	X
United States of America	12.422	N	Merit	11	X	A.3/A.6/A.7/ A.9/A.10	X
United States of America	12.873	N	Merit	12	X	A.1/A.6/A.7/ A.10/T.1	X
United States of America	12.833	N	Merit	11	X	A.1/A.3/A.6/ A.7/A.10	X
United States of America	12.831	N	Merit	11	X	A.1/A.3/A.6/ A.7/A.10	X
United States of America	12.994	N	Merit	11	X	A.1/A.3/A.6/ A.7/A.10	X
Grenada	12.028	PC	Merit	12	A.8	A.6/A.7/A.10/ T.1	X
Grenada	11.765	PC	Merit	12	A.8	A.6/A.7/A.10/ T.1	X
Grenada	12.158	PC	Merit	12	A.8	A.6/A.7/A.10/ T.1	X
Grenada	11.625	PC	Merit	29	O.1/O.3	N.6/N.7/A.6/ A.7/A.10/T.1	X
Grenada	9.207	PC	Merit	5	T.1	A.1/A.5	X
Guatemala	10.626, 10.627, 11.198, 10.799, 10.751 e 10.901	PC	Merit	13	A.1	A.5/A.10/T.1/ NR	X

Country	Case	Case status	Type of solution	Design	Expected and complied with tools	Expected and not complied with tools	Expected tools and no data on compliance
Guatemala	9.111	PC	Merit	29	N.3/T.1/T.8/O.1	N.2/A.1/A.5/A.7	X
Guatemala	11.382	PC	Merit	20	X	N.2/A.5/T.1/T.8	O.3/NR
Guatemala	11.312	PC	Friendly	9	N.3/T.1/T.4	A.5	X
Guatemala	11.766	PC	Friendly	23	N.1/N.2/N.3/N.4/N.6	A.5/T.8	X
Guatemala	11.197	PC	Friendly	9	X	A.5/A.10/T.8	N.6
Guatemala	9.168	PC	Friendly	13	T.1/T.4	N.2/A.5/T.8	X
Guatemala	P. 133-04	PC	Friendly	18	X	N.3/A.5/T.8	N.2/N.5/T.3
Guatemala	10.855	PC	Friendly	29	N.1/N.2/N.3/T.1/T.4	A.5/T.8/O.1	X
Guatemala	11.171	PC	Merit	9	A.1	A.5/NR	T.1
Guatemala	11.658	PC	Merit	5	A.1	A.5	NR
Guatemala	11.422	PC	Friendly	18	N.1/N.2/N.3/T.1	A.1/A.5	X
Guatemala	12.546	PC	Friendly	33	N.1/N.2/N.3/N.4/N.5/T.1/T.6	N.7/A.1	X
Guatemala	12.591	TC	Friendly	2	T.1/T.8	X	X
Guatemala	P. 279-03	PC	Friendly	18	N.1/N.2/N.3/T.1/T.4	A.5	X
Guyana	12.264	N	Merit	12	X	A.1/A.5/A.6/A.10/T.1	X
Guyana	12.504	PC	Merit	17	A.8	A.5/A.6/A.7/A.10/T.1	X
Haiti	11.335	N	Merit	5	X	A.5/A.10/T.1	X
Honduras	11.805	TC	Friendly	5	A.5/A.6/T.1	X	X
Honduras	12.547	TC	Friendly	1	T.1	X	X
Jamaica	11.826, 11.843, 11.846 e 11.847.	PC	Merit	17	A.8	T.1	A.5/A.6/A.7/A.10

Country	Case	Case status	Type of solution	Design	Expected and complied with tools	Expected and not complied with tools	Expected tools and no data on compliance
Jamaica	12.069	PC	Merit	13	X	A.5/T.1	N.5/A.6/A.10
Jamaica	12.183	PC	Merit	17	A.3/A.8	T.1	A.6/A.7/A.10
Jamaica	12.275	PC	Merit	12	X	A.8/T.1	A.6/A.7/A.10
Jamaica	12.347	PC	Merit	12	A.8	A.6/A.7/A.10/T.1	X
Jamaica	12.417	N	Merit	17	X	A.3/A.6/A.7/A.8/A.10/T.1	X
Jamaica	12.418	PC	Merit	29	N.2/T.1	A.5	N.5/A.6/A.7/A.10/O.3
Jamaica	12.447	PC	Merit	7	X	A.3	A.6/A.7/A.10
Mexico	11.565	N	Merit	13	X	N.3/N.5/A.5/T.1/T.8	X
Mexico	11.807	TC	Friendly	5	A.1/A.5/T.1	X	X
Mexico	388-01	TC	Friendly	18	N.3/N.4/N.6/A.1/T.3/T.8	X	X
Mexico	12.130	N	Merit	5	X	A.1/A.5/T.1	X
Mexico	P. 161/02	TC	Friendly	18	N.3/N.6/A.6/A.10/T.1/T.8	X	X
Mexico	11.822	PC	Friendly	13	N.2/N.3/T.1	A.5/T.8	X
Mexico	12.228	PC	Merit	8	A.3/A.8	A.5/T.1	X
Mexico	12.642	PC	Friendly	13	N.2/N.3/T.1/T.8	A.5	X
Mexico	12.623	TC	Friendly	8	A.1/A.3/T.1/T.8	X	X
Mexico	12.660	TC	Friendly	6	N.6/A.8/T.1	X	X
Mexico	P. 318/05	TC	Friendly	23	N.2/N.3/A.5/A.6/A.7/T.1/T.8	X	X
Mexico	12.551	PC	Merit	49	N.2/N.3/T.1/O.1	N.4/N.5/N.6/N.7/A.1/A.5/A.10/T.8	X
Mexico	12.769	PC	Friendly	29	N.3/N.4/T.1/T.8	N.6/A.10/O.3	N.7
Mexico	12.689	TC	Merit	23	N.3/N.5/A.4/A.7/A.10/T.1/T.8	X	X
Mexico	12.813	PC	Friendly	2	T.1	T.8	X
Nicaragua	11.381	PC	Merit	5	T.1/T.6	A.5	X

Country	Case	Case status	Type of solution	Design	Expected and complied with tools	Expected and not complied with tools	Expected tools and no data on compliance
Paraguay	11.506	PC	Merit	6	X	A.5/T.1/NR	X
Paraguay	11.607	PC	Merit	43	X	A.5	N.1/N.2/N.3/ N.6/A.1/A.6/ A.7/A.10/ T.1/T.4
Paraguay	12.431	TC	Merit	4	A.2/ A.6/A.10	X	X
Paraguay	12.358	PC	Friendly	18	N1./N.2/N.3/ A.2	A.5/T.8	X
Paraguay	P.1097/06	TC	Friendly	13	N.1/N.2/N.3/ A.1/T.8	X	X
Peru	11.800	TC	Merit	5	A.4/A.5/T.6	X	X
Peru	11.031	PC	Merit	12	T.1	A.5/A.7/T.8	A.6
Peru	10.247	PC	Merit	12	X	A.5/A.6/ A.7/ T.1/T.8	X
Peru	11.099	PC	Merit	12	T.1/T.8	A.5/A.6/ A.7	X
Peru	12.035	TC	Friendly	5	A.4/T.1/T.4	X	X
Peru	12.191	PC	Friendly	22	T.1/T.4	A.5/A.6/A.7/ A.10/T.8	X
Peru	11.149	TC	Friendly	12	A.1/A.3/T.1/T.4/ T.8	X	X
Peru	12.078	PC	Friendly	8	X	A.1/A.4/A.5/ T.6	X
Peru	P. 185-02	TC	Friendly	9	N.2/A.4/T.1/T.6	X	X
Peru	12.033	TC	Friendly	2	T.1/T.4	X	X
Peru	P. 711-01, P. 33-03, P. 732-01 e P. 758-01	PC	Friendly	23	X	N.2/A.4/T.1/ T.6	A.3/A.6/A.7
Peru	P. 494-04	PC	Friendly	9	T.1/T.6	N.2/A.4	X
Peru	P. 71-06	PC	Friendly	23	X	N.2/A.3/A.4/ A.6/A.7/T.1/ T.6	X
Peru	12.041	TC	Friendly	10	N.6/A.1/T.8/O.3	X	X
Dominican Republic	12.174	TC	Friendly	6	N.5/A.10/T.1	X	X
Trinidad and Tobago	12.269	N	Merit	7	X	A.3/A.6/A.7/ A.10	X

Country	Case	Case status	Type of solution	Desi gn	Expected and complied with tools	Expected and not complied with tools	Expected tools and no data on compliance
Uruguay	11.500	TC	Merit	13	N.2/A.1/A.4/A.7/T.1	X	X
Uruguay	P. 228-07	TC	Friendly	6	N.1/A.7/T.1	X	X
Uruguay	12.553	PC	Merit	7	A.8	A.6/A.7/A.10	X
Venezuela	12.555	N	Friendly	2	X	T.1/T.4	X
Venezuela	11.706	PC	Friendly	9	X	A.6/A.10/T.8	O.1
Venezuela	12.473	PC	Friendly	23	T.1/T.2/T.6	N.2/N.3/N.7	A.6

Analyzing the chart, it is possible to move on to another type of analysis, now on the examined isolated **tools' effectiveness rate**. It is assumed that tools that have a low compliance rate are materially **inappropriate for any and all public policy designs** and, therefore, having a presence in a design, be it friendly or meritorious, numerous or not, increases the chances of total or partial **non-compliance** with the solution.

5.6. Overall tool effectiveness rate

For an overall tool effectiveness rate creation, the percentage of compliance with the tool in each analyzed States' case was not taken into account. For this reason, **the rate is considered as general, and not specific to each country.** It was in the general context of the 207 cases that were processed in the IACHR (according to a report published in 2017) that **the general propensity for compliance or non-compliance with each of the tool analysis was guided.** Even when there was uncertainty about the tool's fulfillment, this data was taken into account[85].

This effectiveness rate fluctuates between **0 and 1**, and the closer it gets to zero, the lower its compliance rate percentage (0%); and the closer it gets to 1, the higher its compliance rate percentage (100%).

As much as the overall effectiveness rate may be impaired when there are sufficient cases of inaccuracy regarding the tools compliance, this option seemed more appropriate than ignoring this number, because an IACHR later report (corrected and updated) may facilitate the indicator's reconformation.

The tool effectiveness rate can be summarized as follows:

$$E: \frac{C}{C+D+I}$$

Legend:
E means the overall tool effectiveness rate (which varies between 0 and 1);
C represents the number of times the tool has been mentioned and fulfilled;
D indicates the number of times the tool was mentioned and not fulfilled;
I means the number of times that the tool has been mentioned, but there is no data on its fulfillment (indeterminacy).

It could be said that there is a **design's material inability presumption** when the effectiveness rate of one (or several) tools is **very far from 1 and very close to 0**. This cannot be confused with the fact that some drawings composed by many tools, divided into several genres, are presumed formally unfit.

It is used the *inability presumption* **expression**, because, as defended in the present model, the ruler can, if he believes it is advantageous to comply with a very complex design (formally and materially), comply with it. So it is just an inability presumption. Furthermore, in Political Science, **there are no cartesian certainties**, but a bayesian probabilistic bias.

The overall tool effectiveness rate is important for two reasons. The first, allows certain **tools' material inability** to full compliance analysis, regardless of the country context in which they will be imposed. It does not take into account its ability to be fulfilled by a certain country or at a certain historical moment; but, rather, **conglobated and protruded in time.**

The second reason is that this rate demonstrates that, although the public policy design's lower numerical complexity may have an influence on these solutions' total fulfillment, it may be relevant to analyze each of the tools in isolation. Anyway, even if it is presumed that a smaller number of tools in the solution design increases its total fulfillment possibility, it must not be forgotten that specific tools - **embedded in a lower fulfillment historical percentage** - can decrease the chances of full compliance with the demand.

Concepts about public policy designs and tools' formal and material aptitude make perfect sense. Designs that contain few tools (**formal aptitude**) and which also provide for tools with an adequate overall effectiveness rate (**material aptitude**) are presumed to be the most likely to fully comply.

The overall tool effectiveness rate is intended to highlight the presumed institutional, legal, political and economic costs for each of the tools' fulfillment. In other words, as expected when analyzing the public policy designs' numerical complexity, the overall effectiveness rate also works as a strong informational shortcut to demonstrate the implementation costs for each tool.

The lower the effectiveness rate, the higher the percentage chances that the costs inherent to its implementation are high and vice versa.

This rate shows that the options for certain tools (in a respective solution design) can increase the chances of full compliance. Measures that have a higher rate of effectiveness are those that means lower costs to government officials and, therefore, have a greater chance of compliance.

It is clear that whoever judges whether it is advantageous to comply with the measures is the ruler. For this reason, the present rate only indicates, in percentage, the greatest propensity to comply (according to each measures' history), but does not provide certainty that they will be complied with. It is an estimate of the costs immanent for its realization, as well as its greater or lesser acceptance by all governments, which is why it is linked to the bayesian bias.

5.7. Public policy categories and overall effectiveness rate

5.7.1. Nodality tools

The first category is **nodality.** This public policy tools category is based on the **use of information** as a vector for the aimed humanitarian purposes achievement. Among the tools possibilities in this category are advertising campaigns, exhortation (or persuasion), benchmarking, commissions and surveys.[86]

However, as already warned, in the inter-American context, some **readjustments** are necessary in the tools that originally make up this genre, due to the stage's specificities on which they will be applied, namely, the Inter-American Human Rights System (organizational field).

After the IACHR case follow-up report thorough analysis, in the nodality category, it was possible to assess the presence of the following common tools in friendly and meritorious solutions.

Chart 6 – Nodality public policy tools [87]

Legend: Comp. - Compliance with the tool among the cases in which it is provided; Non comp. - Non-compliance with the tool among the cases in which it is provided; Imprec. - Inaccuracy cases regarding compliance / non-compliance with the tool among the cases in which it is provided; and Rate- Overall tool effectiveness rate.

Initials	Description	Comp.	Non comp.	Imprec.	Rate
N.1	Publication of the agreement, recommendation or work result in the national and / or local press.	17	7	2	0,6538
N.2	Public statement in the victim's and / or his or her family members name honor, either through the press or by other symbolic form.	27	7	3	0,7297
N.3	Recognition, by public act or formal apology, of the State's international responsibility.	26	6	1	0,7878
N.4	Alteration, modification or creation of subjects, activities or matters in professional training courses' curricula (including police officers).	8	3	1	0,6666
N.5	Promote the public agents' training (including police).	9	6	8	0,39130
N.6	Production of information through studies, meetings, working groups, Truth commissions, action plans (including for carrying out legal reviews).	10	9	2	0,4761
N.7	Disseminate information, through campaigns, academic activities, lectures or similes, with the purpose of exhorting a specific practice with a humanitarian bias.	3	5	2	0,3

It is curious that some of these nodality tools also turn to the victim's public moral reparation or even his relatives', even if in a reflexive way. They also depend on a certain financial contribution to make such information dissemination viable.

These tools' two secondary attributes do not denature its main characteristic, namely, its predominantly informational bias.

Note that tools **N.1**, **N.2** and **N.3** are also characterized by an individual repair load. They come up with a possible consequence of encouraging similar violations' non-repetition, since they can be economically costly for the violating State. Nevertheless, they maintained the prevalence of information as the most startling characteristic.

In fact, a monument construction in a public square can be a good paradigm in this sense. In order to repair the torture and forced disappearances by militarized police forces victims' honor, the violating country's ruler may be forced to build a statue, which will bring financial costs. However, such a measure would still be framed in tool N.2, not least because its main bias is to transmit information (through that symbolic artistic work) about the violations for the whole social group. Only indirectly affects the victims' indirect reparation (through the repulsion for the acts suffered by it public representation), generating economic losses for the State (construction costs).

There are other nodality tools in which the information is directed to certain vector groups, as they are able to disseminate good practices due to the information internalization. In this context, the tools listed in items **N.4** and **N.5** are mentioned. Here, street-level bureaucracy is at the humanitarian intervention's epicenter. A good example of such measures is the curricular grades' modification in training courses and the public agents directly involved in the violation processs' training.

This type of tool is aimed at groups of actors in an attempt that, internalizing the new vectors, build another acting way, using the structuring structures premises.[88] It is a bet on the humanitarian values' informational exhortation, and not on the State's mandatory nature (which is linked to the authority category).

There are also tools in which the information production, through studies or working groups, becomes the end in itself. This includes working groups, truth commissions and even groups to subsidize legislative changes. In this case, it should be noted that the tool listed in item **N.6** (information production) is not to be confused with the tool listed in item A.7 (which is the recommendation for legislative change). It is one thing to determine that information is produced to support the decision on possible legislative changes; it is another to make these law changes happen. The costs involved are presumably higher in the legiferating tool (A.7). This can be seen in the two tools different overall effectiveness rate.[89]

Finally, tool N.7 is a tool that works as a reserve soldier, that is, when no other fits in the specific case, it is called as supedaneous. It is a more open and generic clause, but it has undeniable practical use. This dissemination aims to encourage practices favorable to the human rights 'pillars and, thus, to avoid similar future injuries.

5.7.2. Authority tools

The political instruments based on authority have as a peculiarity the startling **State's empire power** against the state bureaucracy members 'wishes and designs, as well as its administrators'.

Among the tools in this category are command and control regulation, as well as advisory committees.[90] It is obvious that the authority category has also undergone readjustments to suit the present model's needs.

Chart 7 – Authority public policy tools

Legend:

Comp. - Compliance with the tool among the cases in which it is provided;

Non comp. - Non-compliance with the tool among the cases in which it is provided;

Imprec. - Inaccuracy cases regarding compliance / non-compliance with the tool among the cases in which it is provided;

Rate - Overall tool effectiveness rate.

Initials	Description	Comp.	Non comp.	Imprec.	Rate
A.1	Determination for internal bodies or powers to provide information or perform certain administrative acts.	13	41	4	0,2241
A.2	Determination for the internal bodies or powers to restrict judicial remedies against sentences favorable to the violations victims or to close proceedings that are currently being processed against them.	3	0	0	1
A.3	Determination so that the internal bodies or powers create conditions for the victims to appeal or take actions due to the violations suffered, including to obtain a retrial or exercise any of their rights.	10	18	4	0,3125
A.4	Determination for the internal bodies or powers to admit or readmit people (in positions, jobs and functions) and return to enjoy personal advantages.	7	5	0	0,5833
A.5	Determination for the internal bodies or powers to proceed or initiate criminal prosecution (and the sentence execution) in face of those responsible for the rights in question violation, as well as punish those who caused the non-criminal prosecution of those responsible for the violation.	8	91	3	0,0784
A.6	Determination for the national or state Executive Power to regulate laws or propose procedural administrative changes based on their duties.	12	55	16	0,1445
A.7	Determination for internal bodies or powers to create, repeal or reform laws (or adhere to Pacts) seeking to maximize human rights.	13	61	12	0,1511
A.8	Determination for internal bodies or powers to commute, slow down or exempt from penalty (or its effects) a certain person.	12	9	0	0,5714
A.9	Determination for the national constituted Powers to compel internal bodies or organizations to refrain from retaliating or harming the victim or petitioner in any way.	1	2	0	0,3333
A.10	Determination for the Public Power to develop a public policy with a specific purpose.	7	47	13	0,1044

What is common among all tools of this kind is the **State's imposition on public bodies (and its agents) or even on private individuals.** Not that the tools provided for in the other categories do not implicitly bring some command power. In fact, in the authority category, **the regulatory, hierarchical, police and law enforcement powers are placed in a prevalence level.**

The first tool of its kind (**A.1**) evokes a determination for the State (or individuals) to provide certain information, as well as to carry out a specific administrative act. This tool ends up working as a subsidiary clause, when an authority genre's more specific command (provided for in another tool) is not the subject of the recommendation or the agreement. It then functions as reserve soldier for other tools of this kind. There are several examples that can be mentioned here: handing over documents to the rape victim, searching for missing persons' bodies, and deactivating enclosures used for human rights violations.

Tool **A.2**, on the other hand, limits the State's postulatory action (or appeal) against the violations victims 'interests. State bodies are limited in terms of their right to plead something in court, as well as being prohibited from appealing a decision that was favorable to the violation victim. The idea is to satisfy some of the victim's interests (or his legal representative's) by not acting on the State's part in the judicial process, reducing the chances of a favorable decision eventual reform. Certainly, this measure is also adequate to avoid merely delaying resources that eternalize the process for the effective victim's reparation.

Tool **A.3**, on the other hand, determines that the State should take action to enable the resources filing for the reform of an unfavorable decision for the violation victim's right or the petitioners'. It is the reverse of tool A.2, but it goes a little further. In fact, the tool can also be used to ensure a retrial in the victim's favor, in addition to guaranteeing the exercise of any other right recognized for the violation victim.

The tool (A.3) presumably carries a considerable legal cost for its implementation. Perhaps this is why its overall effectiveness rate is relatively low (0.3125). The justification is that, depending on the fact that there has already been national judicial decisions' res judicata, it is not easy to reopen the case internally.

In this case, the res judicata and the very State's right to punish prescriptibility end up being very important. This can be a major problem, as the IACHR itself may be seeking to redress one right by violating another.

It seems that the IACHR may have already noticed this and, as a way out, started to withdraw the State's obligation to **commute the sentence** (A.8). The fact is that, when a new judgment on the case seems impracticable, commuting the sentence appears as a less costly possibility for the government official. In this sense, among several examples, there is the Case 12.504 of Guyana.[91] It should be noted that this other tool (A.8) has a slightly higher overall effectiveness rate (0.5714).

Tool **A.4**, on the other hand, is suitable for those humanistic violations that deal with jobs or functions loss. In this instrument, the ruler is obliged to readmit people, who were unduly disconnected from their activities, and the State is obliged to restore all the advantages related to the status quo ante. What is interesting about this tool is that, when designing the solutions, it is usually associated with the one listed in item T.6, which recommends the assets' payment due to violation (usually values not perceived during the termination period).

The next tool to be described (listed in item **A.5**) is one of the **most important of the authority genre** and, perhaps, of the entire set available. This mechanism brings the imperative for the government to **order the investigation and punishment of the criminal facts that originated the international complaint,** in addition to seeking the punishment of public agents who did not carry out such investigations internally to the satisfaction (for alleged leniency).

In addition to a criminal investigation natural difficulties, there are still corporate strains. Seeking the public agents' punishment (for alleged administrative actions or omissions perpetrated in the exercise of their duties), even if they have already been the target of previous investigations (based on internal legal statutes), in addition to creating friction, **may offend the national legal system**, which usually **do not allow double investigation, prosecution or criminal execution for the same fact** (*ne bis in idem* principle).

It does not seem viable for a citizen to be eternally criminally persecuted for a commited criminal act. The criminal offenses' prescriptibility constitutional guarantee is ensured in most of the Constitutional Letters of the American Convention on Human Rights 'signatory countries[92].

In this way, it seems plausible that the government will be compelled to not comply with the aforementioned tool, since its legal costs are excessively high. After all, it is the government's obligation to go against the national legal system to satisfy an international recommendation, and often the prescription recognized internally prevents this tool implementation. To demonstrate this, see the example of Case 11.605 from Ecuador.[93]

In the same vein, there is still the problem arising from the investigations archiving or even the res judicata in face of the acquittal of those investigated for the violations reported to the IACHR. However, when a **case is decided definitively internally,** investigations and processes **cannot be reopened**, no matter how respectable the IACHR's suggestion may be. Therefore, only on new (substantially new) evidence basis can one speak of reopening an investigation or a case already tried (criminal review); in any case, only if that fact has not prescribed. In this sense, the Brazilian State's justification for non-compliance with tool A.5 in Case 12.001 in Brazil is interesting.[94]

Anyway, these high costs may serve as a potential explanation as to why the overall effectiveness rate of this investigation tool (A.5) is **very low (0.078)**, and, when provided in the case solution design, **the case status is usually of total or partial non-compliance**.

It is possible that this non-compliance with the tool's high rate is due to the lack of legal mechanisms that legitimize public authorities to file new complaints against public officials, especially when they have already been investigated, accused or prosecuted. Another possibility concerns the fact that, as it takes years for the facts perpetrated to the against the victims to reach the IACHR, the probative basis for this criminal offense is likely to have been lost. The probative chance vanishes over the years, as the traces disappear and the witnesses forget the facts details.

There is mention in the IACHR follow-up report itself of some of these reasons' decisive influence (mainly the loss of the probative chance over the course of time factor) for the low compliance rate justification. In this sense, see Argentina's Case 12,324[95], as well as Ecuador's Case 11,783 [96].

Finally, continuing the analysis of the other tools provided for in this genre, we begin to discuss the tool listed in item **A.6**. This instrument initiates a determination for the government official to promote the laws' regulation or to propose procedural administrative changes based on his duties. This tool is often associated with A.7, as the need for regulation often arises when a new law innovates a country's legal system. Perhaps this is why their overall effectiveness rate is equally low: 0.1445 (A.6) and 0.1511 (A.7).

The tool provided for in item A.7 is also of great importance. The institutional costs are more prominent in it. This is because the present model assumes that the **political bargains around the law approval increase the costs inherent to a public policy implementation**. This tool has a very low overall effectiveness rate (0.151)

Evolving a little more in this tools' genre, we discuss the tool **A.8**. Such mechanism determines that the national constituted powers impose on the internal organs or corporations the commutation, easing or exemption from penalty (or its effects) in face of a certain person. This measure is widely used when the background is the death penalty or life imprisonment.

Of the 19 opportunities in which this tool was viewed, in 16 cases it was linked to countries that adopt the death penalty or life imprisonment (Argentina 1 case; Bahamas 4 cases; Cuba 1 case; United States 2 cases; Grenada 3 cases; Guyana 1 case, and Jamaica 4 cases). Only three cases involve countries (Mexico, Uruguay and Ecuador) that do not adopt the death penalty and life imprisonment as a method of sanctioning. It is urgent to say that this measure also includes the removal of the individual's name from the list of culprits (criminal record), as is the case of what was used in Ecuador's Case 12.238, a country that does not adopt the death penalty or life imprisonment as a criminal sanction method.

The **A.9** tool, on the other hand, is quite peculiar, as it contains a commandment of personal non-repetition, which is a little different from other measures that bring a collective non-repetition mechanism (A.10 and generic measures of non-repetition, for example). In tool A.9, the determination is for national constituted powers to compel internal bodies or corporations to refrain from harming the victim in any way, avoiding personal retaliation, especially due to the petitioner having sought international channels.

Another important tool is the one brought up in item **A.10**. Its importance lies in its similarity with the generic measure of non-repetition (NR). In both, the responsibility granting is allowed so that the violating country's ruler **defines part of the public policy design.** What is also similar is that they boast a low overall effectiveness rate, with the NR tool boasting 0.083 and the A.10 tool at 0.104.

The biggest difference between these two tools is that, in A.10 tool, the policy designer (either the IACHR or the parties to the friendly settlement) specifies the object of the public policy to be developed, as well as the possible tools to be used to achieve that determination; on the other hand, in the generic non-repetition measure, the mention is much more vague and broad, either in relation to the object of action, or in relation to the tools to be used. A good A.10 example can be seen in United States' Case 11.331.[97] The NR measure, on the other hand, can be seen in Guatemala's Case 11.382.[98]

It is concluded that **A.10** tool brings a **tied grant**, and the **NR** measure brings a **discretionary grant**. Therefore, while in tool A.10 there are some limits (objective links to be met), in the generic non-repetition measure the design that can be performed by the government is much more elastic and discretionary, as noted in Brazil's Case 11.556.[99]

What is also common is that A.10 and NR tools should target an undetermined beneficiaries group, and should not be restricted to petitioners. If there is a determination of which person (or delimited group) will benefit from such measures, there is no need to talk about the incidence of any of these two tools, as in the United States' Case 11.204.[100]

The division of these two tools into different classifications and different genres aims to demonstrate that, often, one has more objectivity than the other. The non-repetition generic measures' abstraction degree is somewhat strange; they seem more like programmatic measures, than something to be effectively accomplished by the government. This, also, ends up being perceived in their general effectiveness rates' small variation: the NR measure shows 0.083 and the A.10 tool shows 0.104. Regardless, in the end, the result of these two forms of granting responsibility on the public policy design does not have very different effects.

5.7.3. Treasure Tools

The treasure tools have the peculiarity of using the **nation's wealth** as a way of solving the problems that motivated IACHR's humanist intervention.

Through an IACHR's case follow-up report, as well as petitions to submit agreements for the Commission's approval, exhaustive study, it is possible to assess the presence of various tools of the treasure genre.

Chart 8 – Treasure public policy tools

Legend: *Comp.* - Compliance with the tool among the cases in which it is provided; *Non comp.* - Non-compliance with the tool among the cases in which it is provided; *Imprec.* - Inaccuracy cases regarding compliance / non-compliance with the tool among the cases in which it is provided; and *Rate* - Overall tool effectiveness rate.

Initials	Description	Comp.	Non comp.	Imprec.	Rate
T.1	Determination to the internal bodies or powers to pay, immediately, compensation to the victims or their families.	88	47	13	0,5945
T.2	Determination to the internal bodies or powers to pay compensation, in installments, to the victims or their families.	2	0	0	1
T.3	Determination to the internal bodies or powers to pay a death pension to the victims' representatives or relatives.	2	0	1	0,6666
T.4	Determination so that the internal bodies or powers promote exemption from taxes or fees due to the indemnities paid.	39	3	1	0,9069
T.5	Determination for the internal bodies or powers to create an *Ad hoc* Court to set an appropriate value for the indemnity given to the victims and / or their family members.	3	3	0	0,5
T.6	Determination for internal bodies or powers to pay the violation assets.	9	5	0	0,6428
T.7	Determination for internal bodies or powers to order internal bodies or institutions to grant retirement to the victim or his family.	0	0	0	0
T.8	Determination so that the internal bodies or powers grant material or financial conditions for the educational and professional training of the victim (and / or their family members), and / or also provide housing or health treatment to them (and their family members).	23	21	0	0,5227
T.9	Determination for internal organs or powers to impose fines as a measure to correct humanitarian distortions.	0	0	1	0

One point needs to be clarified: as much as most of the tools in this model assume the values expenditure, they should not be placed in this economic category. Unlike these other categories (which also cost money to implement), [101] capital here plays the main vector role for changing that reality. In short, **the treasure genre does not treat money as a mere instrument to realize other intentions; in fact, the wealth transfer is the tool itself.**

To exemplify this, imagine that the IACHR recommends that the State promotes training lessons for police officers, due to the repeated acts of violence practiced by them. It is known that this will entail expenses, but in the end, what matters most in this tool is not the money spent, but the public agents 'convincing through the information that will be given. Therefore, information is the main object of the desired changes. In this example, the educational measure is one of those listed in the nodality list, and not in the treasure genre.

In contrast, the IACHR could recommend that the State pay compensation to the violation victim or to a close relative (petitioner). Here it is possible to notice that money plays a central role in providence, which allocates such measure (indemnity) in the treasure category.

It is important to say that, in their original idealization, the NATO model tools restricted, as a rule, the treasure genre to economic transfers, which encouraged, through subsidies or financial disincentives, a certain positive or negative performance from the bodies or people.

> *These transfers can serve as incentives or disincentives for private actors to follow the government's wishes. The transfer compensates or penalizes and thus stimulates or discourages a desired activity, thus affecting the calculations that social actors make about the costs and benefits of the various alternatives.*[102]

In these NATO model traditional patterns, this category contained the following tools: subsidies, financial disincentives and financing.

Despite the above, the inter-American NATO model brings peculiarities that require a tools species and categories 're-adjustment in order to meet the Inter-American System's peculiarities.

Although indemnty is a form of victims or their close relatives (petitioners) reparation, it should not be forgotten that **they also aim at discouraging similar violations**, mainly by the state budget's direct bleeding. Certainly, in a fiscal austerity time, the risk of limiting the national budget can be a strong incentive to avoid violating human rights. For this reason, we see a double bias in treasure tools: discourage (due to the risk of economic cost) similar violations and repair the violation victim (or legal guardians).

It is important to mention that treasure measures are not

the ones that impose the greatest limitations on government officials and, perhaps because of this, they have **a moderate overall effectiveness rate**. In this sense, it is curious to note that the T.1, T.2 and T.5 tools have general effectiveness rates, respectively, of 0.5945, 1 and 0.5. This indicates that the chance of fulfilling one of these tools is 50% or more.

While money has not lost its importance for the government, it is clear that tools from other categories (not related to the treasure genre) seem to have *higher* implementation costs than it does. **The other costs (institutional, legal and political), depending on the context, exert a greater weight in government decision-making than the economic path, especially with regard to the decision not to comply with the designs.**

That said, let's look at this genre's tools.

The **T.1** tool differs from the **T.2** tool only because the indemnity must be paid in installments in the latter, while in the first one the repair is paid in one installment. This difference is of practical relevance. Because payments in the T.2 tool are deferred, the full compliance status with the case is postponed due to the nature of the measure.

In short, the State, despite of wishing to pay off its obligations quickly, is obliged to wait for the indemnity installments' total payment, and only then will appear as total compliant with that measure. This makes this measure relatively unsuitable for those countries that wish to quickly fulfill their obligations.

For countries with limited budgets (which seems to be a current reality in most of the bloc's states), measure T.2 ends up being advantageous, as it avoids the immediate and total impact on the budget. Therefore, comparing the two tools, this discharge's deferral can be interesting for the government, since it can dilute the payment responsibility with eventual successors.

The IACHR often provides this specific type of tool, which depends on a prudential timeframe[103] to be implemented. This is what the Commission adopts **as tools for successive or time-**

sensitive treatment. It should be noted that these are inadequate tools for government officials who want a certain solution's quick fulfillment, be it friendly or meritorious.

As these two tools (T.1 and T.2) have advantages and disadvantages, some equivalence is expected in relation to their effectiveness rates. Wich didn't happen probably because the T.2 tool sampling was reduced (only 2 cases), with the T.1 tool being linked to many cases (148).

As far as the **T.3** tool is concerned, it is about paying a death pension to the victim's family members, which ends up generating the supposed dilemma mentioned in tool T.2, namely, that of a successive treatment tool. This, however, did not drive the overall rate of such a tool to such low levels. Despite being linked to a small sample (3 cases), the overall effectiveness rate remained at 0.666.

With regard to tool **T.4**, it is important to say that the Commission's (and also the Inter-American Court of Human Rights') understanding is that it is impossible to levy taxes in face of the indemnities paid as such bodies 'performance result.[104]

Thus, the determination for the internal bodies to promote the **exemption of taxes or fees in face of the indemnities paid** is revealed as an almost tautological tool. However, it deserves to appear as an autonomous instrument because there are specific costs for the government to prevent indemnity values 'taxation, with limitations on internal institutions. Exemptions are usually only granted by law and suffer serious constitutional restrictions, as in Brazil's case, whose Constitution (Article 151. III) prohibits the Union from instituting tax exemptions within the States', the Federal District's or the counties 'jurisdiction. Despite that, the compliance level with tool T.4 is extremely high (0.9), which indicates that such costs are not impediments.

Continuing the treasure genre's analysis, the tool listed in item **T.5** deserves further details. It is a determination for the national constituted Powers **to constitute an ad hoc court set an appropriate value for the indemnity given to the victims** and / or their family members. Here the procedure seems a little more complex than the indemnty payment's direct determination, since it is necessary to fix the indemnity amount through the deliberation of a special council created for that purpose. This measure is extremely adequate, due to the fact that it allows the violating State to also be part of this arbitration.

This measure does not bring high costs to be implemented, because the internal wear and tear to reach consensus on the repair values does not match the cost to determine whether an indemnity needs to be paid or not by the violating State. It should be noted that the merit of granting or not indemnity is not considered, but just the value. This makes the measure less dependent on consensus, reducing the institutional cost.

Although the T.5's overall effectiveness rate (0.5) was slightly below the T.1's (0.5945), the difference between the tools can be explained by the **6 mere measure's application cases**. It is possible that, if the sample were larger, the effective compliance with the measure in question would be even closer to the T.1 tool rate.

Another interesting point of this tool is that it was used only in friendly solutions in Argentina. The cases are as follows: 12,080, 12,298, 12,159, 12,182, 12,532 and Petition 21/2005. It's important to stress that in the first three cases cited, this measure was complied with; in the last three there was no compliance.

Tool T.6, on the other hand, determines that the constituted national Powers pay assets resulting from humanitarian violation. This is another technique with a good overall effectiveness rate (0.6428). It is not restricted to joint application with A.4 tool, but it is not uncommon to see them associated. Remember that A.4 is commonly linked to those violations that deal with jobs or functions loss. In it, the State is obliged to readmit people unduly disconnected from their activities, and even to restore all the advantages related to the previous status.

However, the T.6 tool goes a little further. One of the benefits concerns the possibility of repairing meta-individual damages, such as environmental violations. In Belize's Case 12.053, such an instrument was used to repair the environmental damage caused by logging concessions.[105]

T.7 tool deals with the determination for the government official to grant retirement to the violation victim or to his family members. This tool did not impact the mentioned cases in the IACHR report, since the victims (or the petitioners) may be receiving these amounts for other purposes, such as, for example, the indemnty payment. Therefore, the importance of building a set of ideal types, which makes all tools in the specific case's application unnecessary.

The **T.8** tool is undoubtedly one of the most common in the public policies recommended or agreed within IACHR's scope design, depending on the Commission's follow-up case report. Through it, the ruler is obliged to determine that material or financial conditions are created for the victim's (and their families') educational and / or professional training, and grant housing or health treatment to them and their families.

It aims at the victim's reparation and assistance to his close family members, or social group in which he is inserted, seeking conditions for the dignity restoration, giving them fertile ground for reintegration into society. Its overall effectiveness rate is similar to that of the other indemnity measures (0.5227).

Sometimes, this tool ends up suffering from the same dilemmas as deferred treatment measures (postponed in time), which makes the solution fulfillment stay pending for too long. An example is the maintenance of T.8 tool's the partially fulfilled status while a student remains receiving the scholarship. This, in fact, is what is narrated in Mexico's Case 11,822.[106] Anyway, note that the overall effectiveness rate is not low, because, as seen, the compliance with the measure's dispersion is a possible attractive for governments with budgetary limitations.

The tool listed in item **T.9** requires the government to impose administrative fines to correct humanitarian distortions. This measure is interesting, as it highlights the State's administrative powers'(police power) self-enforcement capacity, without the necessary intervention by the Judiciary.

Knowing the existence of administrative rules that allow the illegal conduct's sanction by administrative fines, the ruler is obliged to determine that such financial sanctions are applied in order to confer the desired humanistic turn.

This tool has great potential to be widely used in agrarian conflicts context, in which there is the possibility of imposing fines for the inhumane working conditions' imposition. This command does not determine the fine value to be imposed by the State on the violator, but that the government impose the application of such legal mechanisms to discourage a determined violation situation.

Another important observation is that this money will not come from public coffers, but from the rights violator's patrimony. There is only one case in which the tool was applied: the friendly settlement that occurred in Brazil's Case 11,289,[107] and it was not fulfilled. The tool's overall effectiveness rate is 0, a number that derives from the high legal costs to impose a legal sanction on a private individual. There are internal rules that may not allow it, especially due to the lengthy time course (prescription or decay, for example) since the violation.

5.7.4. Organization tools

The tools based on the organization genre are rarely applicated in the context under analysis. Its main object is the public bodies / organizations creation, the public machinery reorganization (direct, indirect and para-state administration), as well as eminently private organizations creation, provided that such administrative engineering acts are aimed at achieving the humanitarian protection objectives.

Chart 9 – Organizational public policies tools

Legend: *Comp.* - Compliance with the tool among the cases in which it is provided;*Non comp.* - Non-compliance with the tool among the cases in which it is provided; *Imprec.* - Inaccuracy cases regarding compliance / non-compliance with the tool among the cases in which it is provided; *Rate* - Overall tool effectiveness rate.

Initials	Description	Comp.	Non comp.	Imprec.	Rate
O.1	Determination for internal bodies or powers to create bodies or departments to investigate, monitor and / or prevent human rights violations, whether by law or by an Executive's act.	4	4	3	0,3636
O.2	Determination so that the internal bodies or powers create positions, to be filled by public tender, whether given by law or by an internal administrative act.	1	1	0	0,5
O.3	Determination for the internal bodies or powers to readjust, strengthen, relocate or reformulate bodies, workers, institutions and departments, whether by law or by an internal administrative act.	5	3	4	0,4166

The focus here is not on the State's intervention on the economic domain (which is perfectly defensible), but on the possibility for the State **to organize and reorganize its agencies and corporations** and, in this sense, carry out a revamped activity when comparing to the previous one that was being provided. All of this, obviously, permeated by the undeniable interest in avoiding humanitarian violations.

Regardless of whether these tools are inserted in a different category from the treasure, they are also **able to bring budgetary commitment**. Not only that; they have a moderate institutional cost. After all, the organizations 'and agencies 'reorganization usually requires to change the actual rules, which causes resistance even from groups affected by the changes.

Creating a new body, which can compete with already existing attributions, brings internal resistance by the conservative bureaucracy (in the Weberian sense), as well as demands an equal power (institutions) distributive norms rearrangement. This, of course, is reflected in the compliance rate with such measures.

For example, the overall effectiveness rate of the O.1 tool was set at 0.363, O.2 at 0.5 and O.3 at 0.4166. These indices maintain a certain reasonability degree in their grading, since creating a body (O.1) is hypothetically more costly than readjusting an existing one (O.3). As for job creation, the sample is so small that it is difficult to have a clear understanding of its costs. In any case, creating positions (O.2) does appear to be less difficult than designing bodies.

The tool represented by the initials **O.1** brings the determination for the government to create bodies or departments to monitor and prevent human rights violations, whether by law or by an Executive's act. It does not matter whether the state entity will have a public or private legal nature, or even if it will be conducted by the State or by the interested population itself. The command is to institute a body that, undeniably, will play an important role in the human rights context (preventing, investigating or monitoring violations of such rights), whether part of the state structure itself or not.

What is curious about this tool is the possibility of using or creating entities by the State, but with an **eminently private bias**. In this sense, it materializes a type of State's reflexive intervention, which acts by promoting (through bodies creation) a type of community self-management. In the IACHR's case follow-up report, it is possible to see the creation of institutions (often foundations) with the objective of later being handed over to the popular administration.[108]

The **O.2** tool, on the other hand, determines that the ruler must **create positions** to be filled by public tender, whether given by law, or by an internal administrative act. It is logical that it should not be just any position, but only those that is related to the need of protecting human rights.

Finally, tool **O.3** determines that the ruler **readjust, strengthen, relocate or reformulate** bodies, workers, institutions and departments, whether given by law or by internal administrative measure.

5.7.5. Generic non-repetition measures

It was essential to create, from the observation of a generic determination that had been used in the inter-American context, a new genre among those original ones.

When analyzing the cases mentioned in the IACHR's follow-up report, **generic mandatory expressions** were mentioned in more than ten opportunities, which give the government the **freedom** to choose the most appropriate tools to avoid **repeated humanitarian injuries**.

Chart 10 – Generic non-repetition measure public policy tools

Legend:
Comp. - Compliance with the tool among the cases in which it is provided;
Non comp. - Non-compliance with the tool among the cases in which it is provided;
Imprec. - Inaccuracy cases regarding compliance / non-compliance with the tool among the cases in which it is provided;
Rate - Overall tool effectiveness rate.

Initials	Description	Comp.	Non comp.	Imprec.	Rate
NR	Determination for the government official to adopt any other tools - or tools set - (regardless of the gender they are inserted in) to avoid further future humanitarian injuries.	1	9	2	0,0833

It is a **type of carte blanche,** in which the ruler needs to carry out a part of the agreed or recommended public policy design by withdrawing his discretion. In this responsibility transfer to the ruler, he can adopt any of the tools (regardless of the gender that are inserted), as long as they seem more appropriate to avoid new humanitarian injuries (discretionary grant).

It was decided to classify this measure, at the same time, as a public policy tool and a type of action. First, because it is listed as a concrete measure to be adopted (tool); second, because it encompasses, as a generic commandment, other more specific and consequent measures (gender).

This measure, although interesting, leaves the public policy design a little more imprecise, as occurred in Guatemala's Case 11.382.[109] It is a fact that such measures do not escape the generality and lack of taxation allegation. The worrying abstraction degree stands out, as shown in Paraguay's Case

11.506.[110]

It is perceived that **this type of commandment is too open,** which brings it closer to a **values' exhortation** than something that can be objectively concretized by the government, a finding reached by examining Guatemala's Case 11,658[111]. If this more elastic construction can guarantee greater flexibility in terms of its suitability in the specific case, it also has the ability to raise the government's insecurity in terms of its full compliance IACHR's analysis.

Finally, in the generic non-repetition measure, **imprecision and generality** are striking characteristics. Along this line is the Brazil's Case 11,556.[112] The abstract and generic mention of avoiding a certain human right or guarantee violations (considered in gender and as an abstractly considered right) does not allow the government to make a clear analysis of its costs, benefits and even its fulfillment..

One of the differences between such measures and A.10 tool is, the commandment's precision and taxativeness. For example, determining the life protection through any measures appropriate to the case is different from striving for life protection through death penalty extinction. The first would be subsumed in the A.10 measure, the second hypothesis being an example of a generic non-repetition measure (NR).

In other words, A.10 tool's great conceptual mark is that policy design (whether the IACHR or the parties to the friendly settlement) ends up outlining the public policy object to be developed, as well as the possible tools to be used in this tied grant; on the other hand, in NR, the mention is much more vague and generic, either in relation to its object or in relation to tools.

The cleavage between these two tools allows us to investigate whether this **lack of gradual objectivity** can lead to even lower effectiveness rates. This hypothesis seems to be strengthened since A.10 tool has a slightly better rate (0.104) - even though it was provided in about 60 opportunities - than the generic non-repetition measure (0.083), which was provided in just 10 cases.

5.7.6. Public policy designs' complexity

It was agreed that the tools matter for the designs 'success or not, even if analyzed in isolation; now, what we want to demonstrate is that the whole work (design) can matter even more. That is why one of the hypotheses is that this designs 'numerical complexity has a negative impact on the government's decision to comply with such measures.

The seminal question is to clarify whether a greater **tools combination** in design has scientific relevance to determine the solution's total compliance rate, be it friendly or meritorious.

The first point to be highlighted is that the primary substrate for the design complexity classification (formal aptitude) are the 5 public policy tools categories used in the solutions design within the IACHR's scope (nodality, authority, treasure, organization and generic non-repetition measures). The main task is to create a **scale in which this measurement relates the total number of tools used against the number of categories in which they fall.**

For measuring the design's formal complexity, none of the public policy tools are given greater weight, taking into account that each one carries varied (and implicit) costs for its implementation, which can be enhanced or reduced according to the context in which the ruler is intermingled. Regarding all tools' assumed immanent costs, remember what was said about the overall effectiveness rate.

Thus, in assessing the design's supposed formal aptitude, one does not question why, for a given government official, the biggest problem is to convince the Legislature to pass a law, and for others the biggest problem is the money to pay for a indemnity.

In designs with the same number of tools, the scaling follows the number of categories in which they are distributed. In this case, **a greater genders' diversity is a factor indicating**

slightly greater complexity, assuming the costs prevalent in each of the genders' heterogeneity. Anyway, the formula gives precedence to the largest number of tools used in the design due to the number of genres in which they are divided.

Chart 11 – Tool complexity, numerical classification and recurrence

Design complexity's increasing numerical classification	Design's composition according to the number of tools x number of the Inter-American NATO model categories	Number of times such a design was found in the IACHR report
1	1X1	7
2	2X1	8
3	2X2	8
4	3X1	7
5	3X2	22
6	3X3	6
7	4X1	6
8	4X2	42
9	4X3	12
10	4X4	1
11	5X1	6
12	5X2	17
13	5X3	18
14	5X4	0
15	5X5	0
16	6X1	0
17	6X2	6
18	6X3	13
19	6X4	2
20	6X5	1
21	7X1	0
22	7X2	1
23	7X3	7
24	7X4	3

Design complexity's increasing numerical classification	Design's composition according to the number of tools x number of the Inter-American NATO model categories	Number of times such a design was found in the IACHR report
25	7X5	0
26	8X1	0
27	8X2	0
28	8X3	1
29	8X4	7
30	8X5	0
31	9x1	0
32	9x2	0
33	9x3	1
34	9x4	1
35	9x5	0
36	10x1	0
37	10x2	0
38	10x3	0
39	10x4	1
40	10x5	0
41	11x1	0
42	11x2	0
43	11x3	1
44	11x4	1
45	11x5	0
46	12x1	0
47	12x2	0
48	12x3	0
49	12x4	1
50	12x5	0
51	13x1	0
52	13x2	0
53	13x3	0
54	13x4	0
55	13x5	0

From the ranking shown, the 3x1 ratio indicates that the drawing had three tools, all of which are arranged in the same category (for example, 3 tools in the nodality category). The 3x3 ratio indicates that there are three tools in the design, each of them in a different genre (for example, one in nodality, one in authority and one in treasure). In this bias, the methodology assumes that the 3x3 design, despite having the same number of tools as the 3x1 design, is more complex and, therefore, brings higher costs for its effectiveness. Therefore, if the **increase in the number of genres increases the complexity**, the 3x3 function is on an ordinal numerical scale of greater complexity than is the function for the 3x2 design and, therefore, the 3x1.

The more complex the design, the greater its implementation costs and, therefore, the greater its supposed formal ineptitude. This attribute is presumed, since the government may well implement any designs that it believes to be advantageous, even those that are extremely numerous and complex. Therefore, it is important to emphasize that very complex designs have a greater probability - by a Bayesian bias - to formal inaptitude.

5.8. Timelessness and independent variables

The decision to comply with the measures protrudes over time, including passing through the hands of several different governments. Hence, it is assumed that **each and every incumbent rational makes the same type of expected utility calculation about such compliance**, which homogenizes the research in a central element: these public agents' strategic-rational decision making.

The cases that are being processed at the International Human Rights Commission, which were used to parameterize the model, refer to legal demands that are being processed in the last 15, 20 and even 30 years.

Although the report is restricted to the procedures that

have been processed by the Commission in recent years, this does not indicate that the facts are contemporary to the process that has been applied at the IACHR. It must be remembered that violations, in order to be presented to the Commission, must have been neglected by the violating countries 'responsible authorities, which necessarily implies a reasonable time passage.

Another point is that the substantive changes in the research variables' occurrence were not noticed, in such a way as to justify the independent variables continuous-time research accompanied by the corresponding numerical update. This was only possible because it was noticed **a small incremental changes historical scenario**, but nothing that requires further research on these oscillations. That is why the unaltered use of data about independent variables was the methodological option. For example, information, such as GDP, did not vary much over the research's time or, when it did, maintained a certain oscillation proportionality compared to the other countries, which does not affect the research core.

Other independent variables management have received the same treatment, as does the nominal categories regarding the political regimes' freedom degree. Conceptually, discrete time surveys, if well constructed, lead perfectly to almost the same results as those obtained with continuous time surveys.

> Perhaps our models' most distinctive feature, compared to other collective choice analyzes, is the central place attributed to the collective decisions' plurality over time. The analysis is not intended to explain the collective decision-making rules' operation on single, isolated issues. The analytical problem posed is that of examining the comparative rules for available as the theses apply to many decisions distributed over "time". Any rule must be analyzed in terms of the results it will produce, not in a single question, but in the whole set of questions that remains for a conceptually finite length.[113]

5.9. Information organization

Before confronting the information extracted from the

IACHR case follow-up report **(published in 2017)**, it is necessary to carry out a series of treatments on the aforementioned information in order to make it compatible with the present scientific objective.

According to each tool's new typologies, as well as the categories attached to the inter-American NATO model, each of the 207 case solution drawings 'details can be viewed in a systematic way.

For this reason, chart 5 is undeniably the most important, as it is where the **tools** that compose **each of the IACHR follow-up report cases' solutions designs**. There, the tools are assembled according to their **compliance or non-compliance**. In addition, information is provided on the design status (if fully met, if partially met or if not met) and the original **solution form** (friendly or meritorious).

The verification of the most common designs numerical composition guarantees a holistic view of which prevailed. It is interesting to note that designs with many tools do not prevail over others (see chart 11).

It is also necessary to verify whether the **207 solution designs** studied are linked to unitary or federated countries (state form), as well as the country's classification according to the respective political freedom degree (founded on the division carried out by Freedom House, with little adjustment).

The *dummy* variable, regarding the political regime's freedom degree classification, brings together the non-free and partially free regimes, since those did not present a significant number for the statistical crossing. Therefore, about the countries 'respective freedom degree, they are categorized as free or not totally free (information mentioned in charts 2 and 14).

Chart 12 Regime design complexity and classification [114]

Variant	Obs	Mean	Standard-error	Min	Max
Design complexity	207	11.34	8.42	1	49
Regime complexity (Freedom House)	207	71.70	15.35	15	99

Chart 13 – Type of solution

Variant	Freq.	Percent	Comp.
Meritorious	98	47.34	47.34
Friendly	109	52.66	100.00
Total	2 07	100.00	

Chart 14 – Political regime's freedom degree

Variant	Freq.	Percent	Comp.
Not-free or Partially free	97	46.86	46.86
Free	110	53.14	100.00
Total	207	100.00	

Chart 15 – State form

Variant	Freq.	Percent	Comp.
Federation	84	40.58	40.58
Unitary	123	59.42	100.00
Total	207	100.00	

5.10. Hypotheses

The **main benchmark** for comparing this information is the **fully complied status (dependent variable)**. It is assumed that the choosing this paradigm is the most correct, as it investigates whether the chosen variables (conflict resolution form, design complexity, State form and political regime's freedom degree) influence positively or negatively on the achievement of total compliance with the solutions.

In this context, it is imperative to test initially if the **less complex designs (few tools and few categories) increase the chances of total compliance with the solutions.** In addition to seeking confirmation of the relation that, as the drawings become more complex (chart 12), the chances of full compliance with the solution decrease.

Finally, it is important to determine whether, as the design complexity increases, the rate of partial non-compliance exceeds that of total non-compliance. This last hypothesis aims to test the derived conjecture that **the government may also choose to fulfill few tools (even in more complex designs) to escape the total non-complier with the solution status.**

Furthermore, it is necessary to check whether the designs linked to **friendly solutions increase the chances of full compliance** with the solutions. Friendly designs should bring lower costs to the government, since he himself (after evaluating this relation between costs and benefits) agrees with the presence of such public policy tools in the solution design.

The fact is that, due to information limitations, they may end up choosing measures that are difficult to comply with internally. That is why it is not possible to predict, utopically, that all friendly measures will be fully complied with. Anyway, only with data crossing (at a statistical level) is it possible to test the hypothesis about the greater propensity to comply with friendly solutions at the expense of meritorious ones.

Still in this same line of reasoning, it is essential to find out if the political regime's freedom degree increases the propensity to fully comply with the solutions. It is thought that **free political regimes find it easier to adhere to tools coming from IACHR's solutions**, since there few internal resistance (from the voters themselves) against external humanitarian interference. The free countries' own institutions (rules) tend to be more receptive to internalizing these international recommendations.

Finally, it is essential to check whether the State form (unitary or federated) qualifies as a factor that increases the chances of full compliance with the solution. Public Policy Literature [115] advocates that **federated countries have greater difficulties in implementing public policies**, mainly due to the higher institutional costs for doing so. The costs of reaching consensus - due to the existence of more distributive attribution rules - are hypothetically higher in federations than in unitary states.

5.11. Results

The information crossing about the designs complexity, type of cases solution (friendly or meritorious), the status regarding their fulfillment (fully fulfilled, partially fulfilled and pending fulfillment), the regime's freedom degree classification (free or not totally free) and state form (unitary or federated) is capable of revealing very interesting positive relationships.

Chart 16 - Determinants of the compliance type with IACHR solutions [116]

Observations: *Fully complied with is the reference category

*$p<0.10$, **$p<0.05$, ***$p<0.01$ Standard errors in parentheses.

Variant	Type	
	Partially	Not complied
Design complexity	0.13***	0.074
	(0.04)	(0.05)
Type of solution (Friendly)	-2.25***	-4.90***
	(0.53)	(0.95)
Regime classification (Freedom House)	-0.055***	-0.074***
	(0.02)	(0.02)
Regime's freedom degree (Free)	-	-
	-	-
State formula (Unitry)	-0.083	-2.53***
	(0.44)	(0.78)
Constant	5.26***	7.42***
	(1.58)	(2.25)
Observations	207	
Pseudo R²	0.271	
Log. lik.	-135.63	

According to the chart's data, it appears that, as the **solution design** becomes **more complex** (depending on the model shown in Chart 11), the greater the chances of **partial compliance** with the design. Strange, taking into account that the data indicate that as the drawing becomes more complex, the chances of total non-compliance do not necessarily increase. This information relates to the governmental decision-making. Due to an even greater number of tools in the model, there is an increase in the chances that the ruler will choose to comply with one or some of them and, then, avoid the case's total non-compliance.

This government's predisposition to comply with most of the imposed or agreed measures, trying to get rid of the complete non-compliance with the solution status, may indicate that this decision is a more strategic action than the decision for the total non-compliance with the solution.

A dangerous balance can be reached as the Commission is satisfied with the violating State's withdrawal from its expected inertia, a fact that can be accompanied by the unwillingness to create an index or a scale for the compliance with the design's gradual measurement. This conclusion is related to the limited rationality vectors.

Based on the **present model of multinomial logistic regression**, there is a **negative correlation between the design complexity and the full compliance with cases status.** This indicates that, regardless of whether certain tools represent higher hypothetical costs for compliance, the number of tools used in the design impacts even more on the total non-compliance with the case solution.

It should be emphasized that, regardless of the tools'genre or species, this relation is present: **the greater the number of tools, the greater the difficulty of reaching full compliance with the design**. It is a fact that the tools' general effectiveness rate (which has undeniable theoretical importance) cannot be excluded from the explanatory set of the present phenomenon, since it has an explanatory and complementary function in face of the hypothesis here corroborated. This individual rate can help to understand this scientific evidence, including pointing more clearly to the decision of the government official to comply with one (and not another) tool listed in that design, aiming at, at least, achieving partial compliance with the solution status.

Another hypothesis is the greater or lesser propensity for friendly solutions to lead to full compliance with the solutions. Here, the relation is even more significant than the previous one. It should be noted that, regardless of the public policy design, **friendly solutions** are more likely to be **fully complied with**, and **meritorious decisions have a greater tendency to noncompliance (total or partial).** In fact, as you progress from the friendly to the meritorious settlement, a percentage gradation from partial non-compliance to total non-compliance is measured. In other words, meritorious case solutions make total non-compliance with the solution even more likely than partial execution.

In these terms, it is possible to assume that **the friendly settlement allows for a more appropriate solution design for those involved in the inter-American dispute**. This may be due to the fact that the government may choose the most appropriate tools for its internal reality, including those that impose the lowest costs. This design customization is a strong incentive for consensual solutions to tend to full compliance. Not that this always happens, even because it is always possible for the government to choose, uninformed, measures that are difficult to comply with internally.

Furthermore, the political regime's freedom degree, according to Freedom House's categorization, must be tested in the light of the solution's total fulfillment. It is assumed that the variable about the political regime's freedom degree can act as an informational shortcut to visualize a government official's hypothetical costs in deciding whether or not to comply with a particular case solution. It is imagined that this variable would well summarize the immanent costs to break with the violating countries' cultural, legal and institutional traditions.

In this sense, with the cross-referenced information, it is possible to verify that, as the cases are linked to **not so free regimes** (classification that brings together the cases of partially free and not-free countries), the chances that such solutions have the partially fulfilled or not fully fulfilled status increase. It is assumed, then, that cases linked to free countries are prone to a **more receptive position towards the solutions' fulfillment, since this humanistic outlook is consistent with such societies' institutional and ideological pillars**, which can also ensure interesting political results for the self-interested ruler.

On the other hand, in cases linked to less free countries, because there is a hypothetical greater institutional and ideological resistance from government officials to external interference to correct distortions of that kind, there are not so many incentives for complying with the IACHR designs. These rationalist model assumptions end up gaining more consistency with the statistical data. Note that countries that are not free are gradually more prone to partial compliance and total non-compliance.

Finally, it is investigated, in regard to the 207 cases' solution designs, whether the respective State form (unitary or federated) maintains any relation with a greater propensity to fully comply with the solutions. It is expected that **the federated countries, when facing the institutional, legal, economic and political costs,** present greater difficulties for the complete desgin fulfillment. This hypothesis is strengthened by the fact that there is an evident relation, in the inter-American context, between the federated states and the largest territories.

With a larger territory and a larger population, it seems necessary to have a more decentralized administrative organization, which often ends up characterizing and pushing the nation into a federative form. Certainly, **federations require great bureaucratic and power structures, bringing greater obstacles for the institutional consensus achievement.** Anyway, these are the premises of the study, with the need to search for concrete elements (statistically) about this relationship existence or not.

When the data are cross-referenced, this presumption is strengthened, as it is found that cases linked to **federated countries** are more likely to have **total non-compliance** than those linked to unitary countries. Instead, cases linked to unitary countries are more likely to be fully complied with.

This result strengthens the hypothesis that there is less need for institutional and corporate bargaining for a public policy design implementation in unitary countries, due to the lower costs for consensus. The fact that unitary countries, as a rule, have lower GDP is perhaps not the most determining factor here: compliance costs go far beyond money.

CHAPTER 6. SYSTEM CORRECTION MEASURES

IACHR's follow-up report analysis points to a **preponderance of unfulfilled solutions** (wholly or partially) when comparing with fully complied with decisions. For this reason, it seems not only appropriate to investigate the government officials' decision-making rationality about the compliance or non-compliance with the solutions design, as this would not, in itself, lead to improvements in the regional system. It is necessary to see the rationality itself to point out possible directions for the systemic efficiency problem. In this context, there are three possibilities to increase the compliance rate.

The **first possible measure** would be to force the government to comply with the IACHR's recommendations through more forceful **retaliation**. Strength would overcome any need to search for a more communicative bias, making one player much stronger than the other. In this case, there would be a need to engender an reform on the American Convention on Human Rights in order **to allow the State party exclusion from the context of the International Organization**, should it fail to comply with them without reason.

In this scenario, the American Convention on Human Rights (ACHR) should be amended, as currently there is no express provision for this type of sanction. The best way to do this would be to include a provision similar to that contained in the Statute of the Council of Europe:

> Article 8. Any Council of Europe Member who seriously infringes the article 3 provisions may be suspended from his right of representation and asked by the Committee of Ministers to withdraw under the conditions provided for in article 7. If this request is not taken into account, the Committee may decide that the Member concerned no longer belongs to the Council as of a date which the Committee itself sets.

Despite how feasible such a measure is, it appears to be a **drastic and incongruous** alternative in a protection system that **has always been more collaborative than coercive.**

Furthermore, increasing international pressures could unreasonably affect the signatory countries' internal sovereignty and balance and, therefore, internal legitimacy crises could set in.

States are sovereign entities that theoretically have the legal authority to close their borders to any and all external influences, if and when they choose. In reality, however, it is almost impossible for States to stop external influence at the border, because of the restrictions established in the international system. The degree to which a State is able to assert its sovereignty depends on the international pressures' severity and the nature of the issue at stake, as well as on the characteristics inherent to the State itself.[117]

Too much international pressure is always a risk to States, as it can have economic, social and political consequences for internal governance.

In addition, if the possibility of country's exclusion were to become viable, there would be too much strengthening of one of the actors involved in this context, namely the Commission. Excessively strengthening the IACHR's coerciveness would not necessarily contribute to collaborative action among players, which could propel the Commission towards designing recommendations that are less and less concerned with thegovernment officials' socio-economic reality. Hence, the vicious cycle of rigidity and non-compliance could even worsen.

Furthermore, even if this exclusion was allowed, such a measure would not guarantee that the humanistic recommendations would be implemented, nor the previous ones, nor those that could come. In fact, **there would be a possibility that this exclusion would worse the respect for human rights situation in that country,** as there would no longer be the same external pressure opposed to that ruler. This would certainly put the IACHR's own role in the spotlight as a regional system pivotal organ for the human rights protection, since the main protective task would end up being transferred and limited to the national governments expelled from the Inter-American System.

The **second possible alternative** concerns the possibility of fully **transferring** the **responsibility** for the public humanitarian policy design to the violating state's ruler, with the IACHR being responsible for analyzing the effectiveness of the public policies outlined and implemented by the local government. In this case, the Commission would recommend that the governor solve that problem, without fixing the methodology or even the tools that should be used.

As much as this **decentralization appears to be more democratic and therefore more efficient**, this is not believed to be a Solomonic measure. Especially because the IACHR's follow-up report already indicates that **such liberality does not bring as good results as might be expected**, at least in the present moment of American polyarchies' evolution.

A good indication of this is that the two measures to transfer the public policy design's attribution effectiveness, which are listed in the case solutions provided for in the IACHR's follow-up report, bring low compliance rates. The measures are: **A.10**, which is the determination for the Executive to develop a public policy with a specific purpose; **NR** - the generic non-repetition measure, which grants the State the possibility to adopt any measures so that similar humanitarian problems no longer occur.

What is interesting about these two public policy measures is that they provide a grant for the government to implement the tools he believes necessary to meet a certain point in the solution design. However, this discretion did not bring as good results as expected, which goes against the hypothesis brought up in the model that this responsibility granting to the State itself does not have the ability to bring great effectiveness to the inter-American context as one might expect.

Another argument in favor of this solution is that, if the State allowed its action or inaction to trigger petition to the IACHR, this discretion in relation to the design may also be the target of a similar lenient propensity.

Finally, the **third possible route** would be the IACHR's obligation to **consider** its humanitarian public policy designs' **complexity** in the violating country's context, even when the solution is friendly. This shows the importance of showing the positive relationship between the design complexity and the compliance rate with the solutions, based on the recognition that some measures are more difficult to be fulfilled than others.

In fact, **not only does the IACHR need to be aware of these conclusions, but also the parties when they reach an agreement.** The lack of information on the tools' fulfillment (such as those that will be exposed below) can prevent players from realizing the intrinsic difficulties in complying with certain measures.

If it becomes evident that there are more complex designs and tools that are more prone to non-compliance, it can be considered that the IACHR may be playing against its own interests when it continues to develop (or ratify) solutions that do not correct such problems. This stance promotes that the violating country does not comply with the recommendations, and this ends up undermining the IACHR's credibility as a regulatory organization. It is possible that the Inter-American Commission on Human Rights is producing what is conventionally called in the rationalist literature **unintended consequences**.

The most surprising unintended consequences make everyone's situation worse. Sartre referred to this as counter-finality, using erosion as an example. When farmers try to get more land by cutting down trees, they may end up losing land because large-scale deforestation leads to erosion. Counterfinality instances abound. When everyone stands up to get a better view of the game, nobody can and everyone gets tired of standing up.[118]

CHAPTER 7. CONCLUSION

The recommendations and agreements contained in the Inter-American Commission on Human Rights' case follow-up report, contained in the Annual Report published in 2017, were analyzed, depending on the spectrum of their compliance or not by the violating State's rulers.

The governmental decision pattern was verified based on the hypothetical multiple costs that permeate such posture. Therefore, the local arenas' multifactorial study (organizational field) allowed to show a series of restrictions and stimuli related to the rational decision of governments and organizations that play such an international game (IACHR).

That is why proxy variables were essential for the present model of action, as it would be an extremely difficult task to measure all the factors that influence the government's decision. Therefore, due to the natural difficulty of measuring these costs in isolation, it was decided to assume them for the solution design's complexity and the way of solving the demand, in addition to doing so based on relevant internal contextual factors, such as the political regime's freedom degree and the state form.

The main reason for conducting this study was the discovery that there was no work that investigated the relationship between the costs of implementing the public policy tools that make up the solutions held in the IACHR and the government officials' respective rational decisions regarding compliance or not with the designs.

The rational decision-making model shares the assumptions that governments (as well as fundamental rights and guarantees violations victims and the Inter-American Commission on Human Rights itself) always act to maximize their advantages, always at the lowest possible cost.

The limitation caused by transitional mandates is an important explanatory factor in the government's decision-making process. When faced with a very complex IACHR solution and even established in management prior to his, he ends up pondering even more about the costs arising from the risk of internal and external political support loss (political bias), the limitations arising from the fiscal austerity term (budget bias), the difficulty of carrying out an institutional arrangement aimed at implementing the measure (institutional bias) and, finally, even the legal feasibility of adopting that measure (legal bias).

Both in terms of the decision costs and in relation to the model's own tools, ideal types were used to facilitate the fitting of what is provided in the IACHR's follow-up report and what we decided to consider as an appropriate conceptual definition for the institutes.

The existence of standard tools listed in the IACHR's case follow-up report finding culminated in the grouping them into categories and genres, using the NATO model as inspiration. Only after this complicated work of distributing these tools in genera and species, it became possible to analyze the solution design's complexity and, therefore, each measure's overall effectiveness rate.

The presumed costs to implement the solutions, with regard to the tools' complexity and the solution designs, were focused in two main axes: the presumed formal aptitude and the presumed material aptitude of the tools/drawings. The formal aptitude presumption concerns the solution design's complex structure, taking into account the number of public policy tools and how many genres they are divided into. The material aptitude presumption will focus on the type of tools that are being inserted in such a model (mainly those that have a low overall effectiveness rate). Statistical tests will be carried out due to the designs 'supposed formal aptitude in order to confirm the hypothesis investigated here, and the presumed material aptitude will have the character of a mere explanatory complement for this first relation.

It can be seen, therefore, that one of the research's main purposes was to function as an external and informational stimulus, in order to make those involved in the referred international context change their postures.

It was possible to observe the humanitarian public policy designs' nuances coming from the Inter-American Commission on Human Rights, including the way in which they push the government towards compliance or non-compliance. Understanding how and why governments act in this way, as well as what are the factors that contribute to a greater solutions' effectiveness, is an important vector to indicate to the American Human Rights System even more promising directions.

The circumstances that help explain the decision whether or not to comply with a public policy stemming from the IACHR have been demonstrated. Hence the attempt to raise some variables - even if approximate - that represent the implicit costs to which the government decision is linked.

At this point, the complex designs, the case solutionform, the State form and the political regime's freedom degree were chosen as independent variables in order to know if the government's decision to comply with such designs really maintains a relation with such circumstances.

The government official always analyzes costs and benefits and only then decides whether or not to comply with a specific solution from the Inter-American Commission on Human Rights. It is a type of expected utility calculation.

The representative presumably takes into account the following costs: institutional (as is the case with the immanent difficulty in political articulations to achieve a law approval); economic (as is the case with expenses with large indemnties payment); political (political support loss due to the budget prioritization for the realization of humanitarian policies instead of the population's other needs) and legal (the legal and constitutional barriers that prevent the measures recommended by the IACHR's - or agreed with the victim violation -

full application, as is the case of prescription, res judicata, amnesty, as well as the theory of probative chance loss incidence).

The attempt to isolate such costs in hermetic categories has only proved useful for analytical and theoretical purposes. Finally, institutional, political, economic and legal costs are academically independent, but intertwined in the pragmatic world. Especially because it is noticeable that the four types of costs are present in all the the inter-American NATO model's tools, whether to a lesser or greater extent. Therefore, a tool genre refers to the element used primarily to change the desired social reality (information, money, command power, etc.).

These costs' usage should not restrict them to economic values, even though it is known that any tools to be implemented will affect the state budget. It is noted that not always is the economic path that guides the tool's low effectiveness, with an even greater difficulty in the effectiveness of tools that require large institutional and legal arrangements. What indicates this is that treasure tools have a median overall effectiveness rate, and authority measures do not have good rates.

And with such information's usage, it is possible to determine how complex the solution designs linked to each of the 207 cases studied were. All through the association of this information with data on how to solve the case (friendly or meritorious), the State form (unitary or federated) and the political regime's freedom degree (free and not so free).

Such a multifactorial cross-referenced data allows important scientific findings, among them that the small complexity of the public policy designs recommended or agreed within the IACHR's scope has a positive relation with the total compliance rate. On the other hand, it was found that the greater the design's complexity (and its presumed costs, therefore), the lower the chances of full compliance with the solution are.

It is curious that the increase in the design's complexity [is directly related to the partial compliance with the solution. After all, the government official acts strategically and (when he does not intend to fully comply with the solution) chooses to comply with some tools (or none), in order to escape the total non-compliant with the solution status.

It also appears that there are tools that affect more the compliance than others. Here the focus is not on the solution's design as a whole, but on its integral parts (tools). For this, the tools 'overall effectiveness rate plays an essential role. This finding is a good indication that certain tools should not be used indiscriminately in the case solutions'design, as this ends up increasing the chances of non-compliance with them and, therefore, with the solution's designs of which they are part.

The tools 'overall effectiveness rate is something that needs to be better worked on, even to guide more in-depth research on the government's strategic option to comply with one tool (to the detriment of so many others) in case it decides to fulfill only part of the solution, aiming fleeing the complete non-complier status.

Another important indication concerns the hypothesis that, depending on the way in which the case was resolved, there is a greater or lesser propensity to fully comply with the public policy design. With the information cross-reference, elements that relates with the hypothesis that friendly solutions are more likely to be fully complied with, and, in evolving towards a meritorious solution, the greater the chances, respectively, of partial or even total non-compliance emerge. These results are in line with what the theoretical model recommends, which asserts that the participation of those involved in the solution's design enhances the chances of full compliance with the solution, as it is possible that the government may better measure the costs of implementing the tools that will compose the referred design.

Among other variables to assume the costs of implementing the solution designs are the political regime's freedom degree, as well as the violating state's form of organization (unitary and federated).

The State form (federated or unitary) has the ability to represent some costs imposed on the government, which facilitates or hinders the total compliance with the solutions 'design. Especially because a State's form of organization implies a wide range of restrictions and internal stimuli to the political decision maker, namely, the population size, the bureaucracy and country's institutions and the Gross Domestic Product itself (GDP).

In the inter-American context, federated countries tend to have higher GDPs, as well as boasting a larger population and territory, making them more prone to a larger bureaucratic machine and, therefore, placed at higher costs for achieving internal consensus. Therefore, the State form functions as an approximate variable (proxy) when comparing with other possible implicit cost relationships. These embedded derivations are important because they indicate that Federated countries have more relevant institutional, political, economic and legal costs than unitary countries, at least when regarding the subject addressed in this work.

In this sense, it is enlightening to note that, statistically, there is a greater propensity for full compliance when cases are linked to unitary countries, even if, as a rule, they have less money. The federated countries, on the other hand, are less likely to fully comply with the measures, approaching the partial compliance with the solutions more than the total non-compliance.

Regarding the political regime's freedom degree, it can be seen that, as the cases are linked to countries categorized as not so free (sum of partially free and non-free status), the propensity for partial or non-compliance with the solutions design becomes stronger. This indicates that institutional, legal and political costs are lower in free countries and act in favor of internalizing such humanitarian solutions from the Commission; on the other hand, when it comes to countries that are not so free, there seems to be much greater resistance to compliance. The role of democratic and republican ideas underlying freer regimes can be an adequate explanatory factor.

Finally, with all the assumptions, data and conclusions,

one believes that this work contributes to the Political and Legal Sciences, enabling better decisions by government officials in the human rights implementation, and with that the increase in the effectiveness degree of its protection system.

NOTES

[1] HABERMAS, Jürgen, *Direito e democracia: entre facticidade e validade*. Rio de Janeiro: Tempo Brasileiro, 1997, p. 110.

[2] PIOVESAN, Flávia. Direitos humanos e justiça internacional: um estudo comparativo dos sistemas europeu, interamericano e africano. São Paulo: Saraiva, 2013, p. 41.

[3] BONAVIDES, Paulo. *Ciência política*. 10. ed. rev. e atual. São Paulo: Malheiros, 1999, p. 136-138.

[4] HEYNS, Christof; PADILLA, David; ZWAAK, Leo. *Comparação esquemática dos sistemas regionais de direitos humanos: uma atualização*. SUR: Revista Internacional de Direitos Humanos, São Paulo, v. 3, n. 4, jan./jun. 2006, p. 161.

[5] By the year 2017, 19.277 petitions had been submitted to the Inter-American Commission on Human Rights. The data are accessible on the official website: <http://www.oas.org/es/cidh/multimedia/estadisticas/estadisticas.html>. Accessed on: 27 jan. 2018.

[6] GALLI, Maria Beatriz; DULITZKY, Ariel E. A Comissão Interamericana de Direitos Humanos e o seu papel central no Sistema Interamericano de Proteção dos Direitos Humanos. In: GOMES, Luiz Flávio; PIOVESAN, Flávia. O *Sistema Interamericano de proteção dos direitos humanos e o Direito Brasileiro*. São Paulo: Revista dos Tribunais, 2000, p. 62.

[7] GROS ESPIELL, Héctor. *La Convention américaine et la Convention européenne des droits de l'Homme: analyse comparative*. In: Recueil des Cours de l'Academie de Droit International de la Haye, n. 218, 1989, p. 311.

[8] CIDH, Annual Report. Mar. 2017 Available at: <http://www.oas.org/es/cidh/docs/anual/2016/docs/InformeAnual2016cap2Dseguimiento-es.pdf> Accessed in: May 06 2017.

[9] CIDH, Annual Report. Mar. 2017 Available at: <http://www.oas.org/es/cidh/docs/anual/2016/docs/InformeAnual2016cap2Dseguimiento-es.pdf> Accessed in: May 06 2017.

[10] The intervention must be practiced through an international organization (United Nations), of which all countries involved are members. States,

acting individually or collectively, have the right to adopt, in relation to another State that has violated their obligations in the matter, diplomatic, economic and other measures admitted under international law, provided that it is not an armed force. (ACCIOLY, Hildebrando; NASCIMENTO e SILVA, Geraldo Eulálio do. *Manual de Direito Internacional Público*. 15 ed. São Paulo: Saraiva, 2002, p. 133).

[11] CANÇADO TRINDADE, Antônio Augusto. *Direito das organizações internacionais*. Belo Horizonte: Del Rey, 2012, p. 36.

[12] BICUDO, Hélio. *A Comissão Interamericana de Direitos Humanos: funções e atuação*. In: A proteção internacional dos direitos humanos e o Brasil. Brasília: Superior Tribunal de Justiça, 2000, p. 72.

[13] BARROS, Gustavo. Herbert A. *Simon and the concept of rationality: boundaries and procedures*. Brazilian Journal of Political Economy, 2010, vol. 30, n. 3, p. 457.

[14] TSEBELIS, George. Jogos ocultos: Escolha racional no campo da política comparada. São Paulo: Edusp, 1998. p. 46-47.

[15] OLSON, Mancur. *A lógica da ação* coletiva. São Paulo, Edusp, 1999, p. 73.

[16] SIMON, Hebert A. 1990. *Invariants of human behavior*. Annu. Rev. Psychol. 41:1–19, p. 198.

[17] MARCH, James G.; SIMON, Herbert A. *Organizations*. 2 ed. Cambridge: Blackwell, 1993, p. 162.

[18] DAVIS, Morton D. *Teoria dos Jogos*: Uma Introdução não-Técnica. São Paulo: Cultrix, 1973, p. 54.

[19] The internal context is similar to what was defined by Montesquieu by the general spirit of a country. The idea he defended of associating geographic, historical, cultural and legal factors serves as inspiration for the set of research variables' formation.

The things that govern men are natural phenomena - like the climate - and social institutions - like religion, laws, government maxims; they are also, on the other hand, tradition, historical continuity, characteristics of the whole society and what Montesquieu calls examples of past things. All of these things together form the general spirit. (...) There is a general spirit of France, a general spirit of England.

[20] LIN, Nan. *Social capital: a theory of social structure and action*. Cam-

bridge: Cambridge University Press, 2001, p. 187.

[21] LIN, Nan. *Social capital: a theory of social structure and action*. Cambridge: Cambridge University Press, 2001, p. 187.

[22] BOURDIEU, Pierre. *O poder simbólico*. Tradução Fernando Tomaz. 13 ed. Rio de Janeiro: Bertrand Brasil, 2010.

[23] SCHMIDT, Vivien A. *Discursive institutionalism: the explanatory power of ideas and discourse*. Annual Review of Political Science, v. 11, jun. 2008, p. 303.

[24] DONNELLY, Jack. *Universal Human Rights in Theory and Practice*. 3 ed. Ithaca: Cornell University Press, 2013, p. 175-176.

[25] DAVIS, Morton D. *Teoria dos Jogos*: Uma Introdução não-Técnica. São Paulo: Cultrix, 1973, p.16.

[26] COLLINS, Randal. *Quatro tradições sociológicas*. Petrópolis. Editora Vozes, 2009, p. 147.

[27]. ELSTER, Jon. *Ulisses liberto: estudos sobre racionalidade, pré-compromisso e restrições*. São Paulo: Unesp, 2010, p. 213.

[28] PIOVESAN, Flávia. *Direitos Humanos e o Direito Constitucional Internacional*. 15ª ed. São Paulo: Editora Saraiva, 2015, p. 343.

[29] In the Brazilian case, the Vienna Convention on the Law of Treaties was internalized through Decree 7.030 / 09.

[30] SIMON, Hebert A. 1990. *Invariants of human behavior*. Annu. Rev. Psychol. 41:1–19.

[31] HOWLETT, Michael; RAMESH, M.; PERL, Anthony. *Política Pública*: seus ciclos e subsistemas, uma abordagem integral. Rio de Janeiro: Campus/ Elsevier, 2013, p. 85.

[32] ELSTER, Jon. *Peças e Engrenagens das Ciências Sociais*. Rio de Janeiro: Relume-Dumará, 1994, p. 156.

[33] MAYNARD, S. *A evolução do sexo*. São Paulo: Unesp; 2012).

[34] The first behavioral psychology proposition is called **the law of effect**, according to which, if an animal (or man) act is followed by a reward, it is likely to repeat that act or the like. Once a person has learned the act, behavioral psychology is often called a theory of learning. Some animals can also learn by imitation. If one of them sees another performing an act and then obtaining something deemed rewarding, he will likely reproduce the act. Of course, it will stop reproducing it if, in its case, the reward does not come. In all of this we see a fundamental assumption of behavioral psychology: *today's actions*

affect tomorrow's. (GIDDENS, Anthony; TURNER, Jonathan (Org.). *Teoria social hoje.* São Paulo: Unesp, 1999 p. 93).

[35] PUTNAM, Robert D. *Comunidade e democracia*: a experiência da Itália moderna. Com Robert Leonardi e Raffaella Y Nanetti. Rio de Janeiro: FGV, 2006, p. 147-176.

[36] Dados disponíveis em: <http://www.cidh.org/basicos/portugues/d.Convencao_Americana_Ratif..htm> Acesso em: 30 ago. 2020.

[37] BLAU, Peter M. *Exchange and Power in Social Life.* New York: John Wiley & Sons, Inc, 1964, p. 18-19.

[38] DELLA PORTA, Donatella. *Social Movements in Times of Austerity.* Cambridge: Polity, 2015, p. 123.

[39] . DOWNS, Anthony. *Why the Government budget is Too Small in a Democracy.* World Politics, v. 2, n. 14, p. 541-563, 1960, p. 550.

[40] GALDINO, Flávio. *Introdução à teoria dos custos dos direitos* – direitos não nascem em árvores. Rio de Janeiro: Renovar, 2005, p. 204.

[41] SCHUMPETER, Joseph A. *The crisis of the tax state.* In: SWEDBERG, Richard (Org.). Joseph A. Schumpeter: The economics and sociology of capitalism. Princeton: Princeton University Press, 1991, p. 111.

[42] Concisely, it can be said that rights are divided into positive and negative. **Negative rights** correspond to state abstentions, in the sense of tolerating the indivduals' conduct (civil and political rights that materialize the freedom value). **Positive rights**, on the other hand, include material benefits to the population (social, economic and cultural rights that sediment the equality value), which may involve goods, services or rights supply by the Government. This material implementation of the State's service obligations implies the goods and people allocation, and therefore depends on the effective availability **of material and human resource**s and is subject to a possible reserve.

[43] Check chart 8 in item 5.7.3..

[44] DOWNS, Anthony. *Uma teoria econômica da democracia.* São Paulo: Edusp, 2013, p. 546.

[45] DOWNS, Anthony. *Uma teoria econômica da democracia.* São Paulo: Edusp, 2013, p. 549.

[46] SCHMIDT, Vivien A. *Discursive institutionalism: the explanatory power of ideas and discourse.* Annual Review of Political Science, v. 11, jun. 2008, p. 311-312.

[47] HOWLETT, Michael; RAMESH, M.; PERL, Anthony. *Política Pública: seus ciclos e subsistemas, uma abordagem integral*. Rio de Janeiro: Campus/Elsevier, 2013 p. 34-35.

[48] That have in Political Science a different concept from Legal Science, as seen in the item 2.2.

[49] PL 153/2020, available in: <https://www.camara.leg.br/proposicoesWeb/
prop_mostrarintegra;jsessionid=
32FD5A8292C4E565786D6314237439FF.proposicoesWebExterno2?
codteor=1855142&filename=PL+153/2020>. Accessed in 28 jun. 2020.

[50] BUCHANAN, James M.; TULLOCK, Gordon. *The Calculus of Consent: Logical Foundations of Constitutional Democracy*. 2 ed. Ann Arbor: University of Michigan Press 1962

[51] CIDH, Case 12.447 of Jamaica.

[52] LEVITSKY, Steven; ZIBLATT, Daniel. *Como as democracias morrem*. Rio de Janeiro: Zahar, 2018, p. 107.

[53] LAWRENCE, Thomas B.; SUDDABY, Roy; LECA, Bernard. *Introduction: theorizing and studying institutional work*. In: _____ (Org.). Institutional work: actors and agency in institutional studies of organizations. Cambridge: Cambridge University Press, 2009. p. 5.

[54] PIOVESAN, Flávia. *Direitos Humanos e o Direito Constitucional Internacional*. 15ª ed. São Paulo: Editora Saraiva, 2015, p 175-176.

[55] This is one of IACHR's recommendations in Cases 11,286, 11,406, 11,407, 11,412, 11,413, 11,415 and 11,416 in Brazil.

[56] IACHR's recommendation in Case 11,193 in the United States.

[57] SCHMIDT, Vivien A. *Discursive institutionalism: the explanatory power of ideas and discourse*. Annual Review of Political Science, v. 11, jun. 2008, p. 304.

[58] PIOVESAN, Flávia. *Direitos Humanos e o Direito Constitucional Internacional*. 15ª ed. São Paulo: Editora Saraiva, 2015, p. 182.

[59] DOWNS, Anthony. *Uma teoria econômica da democracia*. São Paulo: Edusp, 2013, p. 549.

[60] CIDH, Case 12.534 from United States of America.

[61] Based on the data available at: <https://freedomhouse.org/report/freedom-world/freedom-world-2016> Accessed in: May 20 2017.

[62] Data available at: <https://freedomhouse.org/report/freedom-

world/freedom-world-2016>. Accessed in: May 20 2017.

[63] Grouping technique in nominal binary categories (called a *dummy* variable).

[64] Check the data treatment in chapter 5.

[65] HOWLETT, Michael; RAMESH, M.; PERL, Anthony. *Política Pública*: seus ciclos e subsistemas, uma abordagem integral. Rio de Janeiro: Campus/Elsevier, 2013, p. 67.

[66] We opted for the comparison with the Gross Domestic Product (GDP), due to the approach about the common-pool resource (common-pool resource), as the choice for per capita income seems inadequate.

[67] IACHR, Annual Report. Mar. 2017 Available in: <http://www.oas.org/es/cidh/docs/anual/2016/docs/InformeAnual2016cap2Dseguimiento-es-.pdf> Acesso em: 06 mai. 2017.

[68] HOWLETT, Michael; RAMESH, M.; PERL, Anthony. *Política Pública*: seus ciclos e subsistemas, uma abordagem integral. Rio de Janeiro: Campus/Elsevier, 2013, p. 68.

[69] Confirmation that it will be possible by crossing statistical data in chapter 5.

[70] Orden Ejecutiva SG/OEA. 17/06, Attachment I, D, 7. Disponível em: <https://www.oas.org/es/cidh/actividades/seguimiento/default.asp>. Accessed in Aug. 30 2020.

[71] The report analysis requires months of intense work and research, which is why, even though we know that new reports have already been published, it was decided to keep studying this report. Furthermore, although occasional changes may appear in the most recent data, the tendency is that the absence of radical changes does not impact the conclusions obtained.

[72] That is, after closing this book's data analysis.

[73] "It was decided to prepare information sheets for each case in greater detail than in previous years, which can be accessed through the links available in the two case charts for monitoring recommendations. The Commission considers that, with this methodology for monitoring its decisions, it is possible to make visible the main results achieved in complying with the recommendations based on the information presented by the parties on individual and structural repairs" IACHR's Annual report. Mar. 2019. Available at: <https://www.oas.org/es/cidh/docs/anual/2019/docs/IA2019cap2-es.pdf>. Accessed in: Aug. 30 2019.

[74] "Partial compliance: cases in which the State partially complies with the recommendations published by the IACHR, either because it has only complied with some of the recommendations or because it has incompletely complied with all the recommendations; the cases in which the State has fully complied with all the recommendations made by the IACHR, except for those whose compliance has been impossible". IACHR, Annual Report. Mar. 2019. Available at: <https://www.oas.org/es/cidh/docs/anual/2019/docs/IA2019cap2-es.pdf>. Accessed in: Aug. 30 2019.

[75] Note that the IACHR's follow-up report did not individualize the measures, nor did it name them as public policy tools. This cataloging was performed here using the NATO model as a paradigm.

[76] Tools classification' detailed explanation can be found in item 5.7.

[77] HOOD, Christopher. *The tools of Government.* Chatham, NJ: Chatham House, 1986.

[78] IACHR, Annual Report. Mar. 2017 Available at: <http://www.oas.org/es/cidh/docs/anual/2016/docs/InformeAnual2016cap2Dseguimiento-es-.pdf> Accessed in: May 06 2017.

[79] CIDH, Annual Report. Mar. 2019. Available at: <https://www.oas.org/es/cidh/docs/anual/2019/docs/IA2019cap2-es.pdf> Accessed in: sep. 01 2020.

[80] HOWLETT, Michael. *From the 'old' to the 'new' policy design: design thinking beyond markets and collaborative governance.* Policy Sciences, v. 47, n. 3, p. 187-207, sep.. 2014

[81] HOWLETT, Michael. *From the 'old' to the 'new' policy design: design thinking beyond markets and collaborative governance.* Policy Sciences, v. 47, n. 3, set. 2014, p. 207.

[82] HOWLETT, Michael; RAMESH, M.; PERL, Anthony. *Política Pública: seus ciclos e subsistemas, uma abordagem integral.* Rio de Janeiro: Campus/Elsevier, 2013, p. 129.

[83] In this regard, the IACHR recommendation to Jamaica can be found in Case 12.418: "Adopt the legislative or other measures that are necessary to carry out an exhaustive and impartial investigation of human rights violations committed against Mr. Gayle , to identify, prosecute and punish all persons responsible for these rights violations".

[84] CIDH, Annual Report. Mar. 2017 Available at: <http://www.oas.org/es/cidh/docs/anual/2016/docs/InformeAnual2016cap2Dseguimiento-es-

.pdf> Accessed in: may 06 2017.

[85] Previous work has already been carried out on this effectiveness index and on its tools. In this sense, see: COSTA, Adriano Sousa. RORIZ, João. As recomendações e soluções amistosas da Comissão Interamericana de Direitos Humanos: política, preferência e cumprimento. Revista do Serviço Público. Brasília: ENAP, 2020, no prelo, DOI https://doi.org/10.21874/rsp.v71i3.3786.

[86] HOWLETT, Michael; RAMESH, M.; PERL, Anthony. *Política Pública: seus ciclos e subsistemas, uma abordagem integral*. Rio de Janeiro: Campus/Elsevier, 2013.

[87] CIDH, Annual Report. Mar. 2017 Available at: <http://www.oas.org/es/cidh/docs/anual/2016/docs/InformeAnual2016cap2Dseguimiento-es-.pdf> Accessed in: May 06 2017.

[88] BOURDIEU, Pierre. *O poder simbólico*. 13 ed. Rio de Janeiro: Bertrand Brasil, 2010.

[89] Conforme tabelas 6 e 7.

[90] HOWLETT, Michael; RAMESH, M.; PERL, Anthony. *Política Pública*: seus ciclos e subsistemas, uma abordagem integral. Rio de Janeiro: Campus/Elsevier, 2013.

[91] "Grant effective reparations, including compensation for the ill-treatment inflicted on the Vaux brothers; a new trial of the charges imputed to the Vaux brothers, in accordance with the judicial protections enshrined in the American Declaration, or, failing that, the due revocation or commutation of the sentence".

[92] In Brazil, there are few criminal offenses that are imprescriptible. They are listed in article 5 of the Federal Constitution, but precisely in items XLII, XLIII and XLIV. The other criminal offenses are considered prescriptive, that is, the passage of time (listed in article 109 of the Penal Law) makes punishment impossible.

[93] "The State has not initiated any legal action to investigate, prosecute and punish those responsible for the violations committed against the victim. On the contrary, given the time elapsed to date, the process
would have prescribed due to the 10-year period provided for in the Penal Law from the date of the event or the start of the trial, without a judicial decision, in cases sanctioned with the imprisonment penalty as a murder crime".

[94] "The State reiterated (...) that, according to the State's procedural legislation, the investigation can only be reopened if new facts or new evi-

dence are brought to the attention of the authorities; He adds that the matter was referred to the Fifth Prosecutor's Office, which proceeded to the corresponding review and determined that the investigation should be shelved again, given the lack of new evidence. In this regard, the State reiterated that it has promoted acceptable legal and constitutional measures and norms to disqualify the investigation, however, in the absence of new evidence, it would be impossible to reopen the investigation in the light of the legal possibilities".

[95] "The State explained that, over time, resolving the case became difficult. In turn, the petitioners indicated that the Defender's Office became a plaintiff in the ilegal coercion case and requested a series of evidential measures, which were deferred".

[96] "The petitioner reported that the arbitrary deprivation of liberty could not be investigated due to the time elapsed since the events occurred, which is why the administrative and criminal actions against the justice operators responsible for the judicial delay and against police agents responsible for the illegal detention prescribed. Due to the foregoing, and given the impossibility declared by the petitioner to contact the victim and comply with the corresponding actions' prescription, the petitioner requested the cessation and filing of actions to follow the friendly settlement agreement.".

[97] "Examine their laws, procedures and practices to ensure that any foreigner arrested in any way, detained or placed in preventive detention in the United States is informed without delay of their right to consular assistance and that, coincidentally, the appropriate consulate is informed without circunstances from abroad delay, in accordance with the judicial guarantees of due process and a fair trial enshrined in Articles XVIII and XXVI of the American Declaration".

[98] "That it take the necessary measures to ensure that future violations of the type that occurred in the present case do not repeat".

[99] "Take the necessary steps to try to prevent similar events from occurring in the future".

[100] "Grant *petitioners* effective redress, which includes the adoption of legislative and other measures necessary to guarantee *petitioners* the effective right to participate in their national parliament, directly or through freely elected representatives and on equal terms."

[101] An example of financial costs immanent to other public policy tools

can be seen in Guatemala's Petition 133/2004: "Regarding the preparation of an international responsibility aknowledgment letter, the State stated that the AFP's (Agence France Press) services could not be specified, since COPRE-DEH did not have the financial resources to allow the publication of that letter.".

[102] HOWLETT, Michael; RAMESH, M.; PERL, Anthony. *Política Pública: seus ciclos e subsistemas, uma abordagem integral*. Rio de Janeiro: Campus/Elsevier, 2013.

[103] "The IACHR stresses that the various recommendations made are for the fulfillment of a successive and not immediate treaty and that some of them require a reasonable period of time to be fully implemented. Therefore, the chart shows the current compliance state that the Commission recognizes as a dynamic process". IACHR, Annual Report. Mar. 2017 Available at : <http://www.oas.org/es/cidh/docs/anual/2016/docs/InformeAnual2016cap2Dseguimiento-es.pdf> Accessed in: May 06 2017.

[104] "The payment that El Salvador makes to people subject to this Notary Act is not subject to taxes that currently exist or that may be enacted in the future". IACHR, Annual Report. Mar. 2017 Available at: <http://www.oas.org/es/cidh/docs/anual/2016/docs/InformeAnual2016cap2Dseguimiento-es.pdf> Accessed in: May 06 2017.

[105] "Repair the environmental damage resulting from the logging concessions granted by the State in relation to the traditionally occupied territory and used by the Mayan people".

[106] "Regarding the scholarships topic, the State indicated that Chiapa's General Secretariat of Government has been granting scholarships since 2008 on a monthly basis in favor of the 3 beneficiaries. The IACHR takes note of this information and considers that the State has complied with this measure. In this regard, the Commission notes that, in the present case, the measure includes the completion of the beneficiaries' professional studies. Therefore, the IACHR will continue to monitor this measure..".

[107] "Strengthen the Public Ministry of Labor, ensure immediate compliance with the legislation in force, through the administrative and judicial fines collection, investigation and presentation of complaints against the slave labor practice's perpetrators; Strengthen the MTE Mobile Group; Carry out actions in conjunction with the Judiciary and its representative entities, in order to guarantee the perpetrators' punishment."

[108] In this context, see Guatemala's Case 11.625: "The creation of a foundation that will be called Fundação Maria Eugenia Morales Aceña de Sierra for Dignity "FUNDADIG ", for which the State assumes its constitution's procedures and expenses, registration and recognition of its legal personality as well as a background for its operation ".

[109] "That it takes the necessary measures to ensure that future violations of that type do not occur".

[110] "Take the necessary measures to prevent these events from repeating in the future"

[111] "Promote in Guatemala the principles set out in the "Declaration on the rights and duties of people, groups and institutions to promote and protect universally recognized human rights and fundamental freedoms", approved by the United Nations, and take the necessary measures for the freedom of speech of those who assumed the task of working for the fundamental rights respect are respected and so that their life and personal integrity are protected".

[112] "Take the necessary measures to try to prevent similar events from occurring in the future".

[113] BUCHANAN, James M.; TULLOCK, Gordon. *The Calculus of Consent*: Logical Foundations of Constitutional Democracy. 2 ed. Ann Arbor: University of Michigan Press 1962, p. 116.

[114] Based on information collected in the IACHR follow-up report and information extracted from the Freedom House website on the political regime's freedom degree.

[115] HOWLETT, Michael; RAMESH, M.; PERL, Anthony. *Política Pública: seus ciclos e subsistemas, uma abordagem integral*. Rio de Janeiro: Campus/ Elsevier, 2013, p. 68.

[116] Based on IACHR case follow-up reports, data from Freedom House and other information in the public domain (state form).

[117] HOWLETT, Michael; RAMESH, M.; PERL, Anthony. *Política Pública*: seus ciclos e subsistemas, uma abordagem integral. Rio de Janeiro: Campus/ Elsevier, 2013, p. 85.

[118] ELSTER, Jon. *Peças e Engrenagens das Ciências Sociais*. Rio de Janeiro: Relume-Dumará, 1994, p. 118.

REFERENCES

ACCIOLY, Hildebrando; NASCIMENTO e SILVA, Geraldo Eulálio do. *Manual de Direito Internacional Público*. 15 ed. São Paulo: Saraiva, 2002.

ARON, Raymond. *As Etapas do Pensamento Sociológico*. 4 ed. São Paulo: Martins Fontes, 1997.

AVRITZER, Leonardo. *A moralidade da democracia*: ensaios em teoria habermasiana e teoria democrática. São Paulo/Belo Horizonte: Perspectiva/UFMG's publishing company, 1996.

BARROS, Gustavo. Herbert A. *Simon and the concept of rationality*: boundaries and procedures. Brazilian Journal of Political Economy, 2010, vol. 30, n. 3, p. 455-472.

BENDER, Katja; KELLER, Sonja; WILLING, Holger. *The Role of International Policy Transfer and Diffusion for Policy Change in Social Protection* - A Review of the State of the Art. IZNE Social Protection Working Paper, International Centre for Sustainable Development (IZNE), Bonn-Rhein-Sieg University of Applied Sciences, 2015. Available at: <http://econpapers.repec.org/paper/sauiznewp/1401.htm> Accessed in: 20 jan. 2017.

BERK, Gerald; DENNIS. Galvan. *How People Experience and Change Institutions*: A Field Guide to Creative Syncretism. Theory and Society, v. 38, n. 6, 2009.

BLAU, Peter M. *Exchange and Power in Social Life*. New York: John Wiley & Sons, Inc, 1964.

BICUDO, Hélio. *A Comissão Interamericana de Direitos Humanos: funções e atuação*. In: A proteção internacional dos direitos humanos e o Brasil. Brasília: Superior Justice Tribunal, 2000.

BONAVIDES, Paulo. *Ciência política*. 10. ed. rev. and actual. São Paulo: Malheiros, 1999.

BOURDIEU, Pierre. *O poder simbólico*. 13 ed. Rio de Janeiro: Bertrand Brasil, 2010.

BUCHANAN, James M.; TULLOCK, Gordon. *The Calculus of Consent*: Logical Foundations of Constitutional Democracy. 2

ed. Ann Arbor: University of Michigan Press 1962.

CANÇADO TRINDADE, Antônio Augusto. *Direito das organizações internacionais*. Belo Horizonte: Del Rey, 2012.

COLLINS, Randal. *Quatro tradições sociológicas*. Petrópolis. Editora Vozes, 2009.

COSTA, Adriano Sousa. RORIZ, João. As recomendações e as soluções amistosas da Comissão Interamericana de Direitos Humanos: política, preferências e cumprimento. Revista do Serviço Público. Brasília: ENAP, 2020, in press, DOI https://doi.org/10.21874/rsp.v71i3.3786.

DAVIS, Morton D. *Teoria dos Jogos*: Uma Introdução não-Técnica. São Paulo: Cultrix, 1973.

DAHL, Robert Alan. *Poliarquia*: participação e oposição. São Paulo: Edusp, 1997.

DELLA PORTA, Donatella. *Social Movements in Times of Austerity*. Cambridge: Polity, 2015.

DONNELLY, Jack. *Universal Human Rights in Theory and Practice*. 3 ed. Ithaca: Cornell University Press, 2013.

DOWNS, Anthony. *Why the Government budget is Too Small in a Democracy*. World Politics, v. 2, n. 14, p. 541-563, 1960.

DOWNS, Anthony. *Uma teoria econômica da democracia*. São Paulo: Edusp, 2013.

ELSTER, Jon. *Peças e Engrenagens das Ciências Sociais*. Rio de Janeiro: Relume-Dumará, 1994.

ELSTER, Jon. *Ulisses liberto: estudos sobre racionalidade, pré-compromisso e restrições*. São Paulo: Unesp, 2010.

GALDINO, Flávio. *Introdução à teoria dos custos dos direitos – direitos não nascem em árvores*. Rio de Janeiro: Renovar, 2005.

GIDDENS, Anthony; TURNER, Jonathan (Org.). *Teoria social hoje*. São Paulo: Unesp, 1999.

GOMES, Luiz Flávio; PIOVESAN, Flávia. O *Sistema Interamericano de proteção dos direitos humanos e o Direito Brasileiro*. São Paulo: Revista dos Tribunais, 2000.

GROS ESPIELL, Héctor. *La Convention américaine et la Convention européenne des droits de l'Homme: analyse comparative*. In: Recueil des Cours de l'Academie de Droit International de la

Haye, n. 218, pp. 167-411, 1989.

HAYEK, F. A. The Road to Serfdom. Londres: Routledge and Kegel Paul, 1976.

HEYNS, Christof; PADILLA, David; ZWAAK, Leo. *Comparação esquemática dos sistemas regionais de direitos humanos: uma atualização.* SUR: International Journey on Human Rights, São Paulo, v. 3, n. 4, p. 161-162, jan./jun. 2006.

HOOD, Christopher. *The tools of Government.* Chatham, NJ: Chatham House, 1986.

HOWLETT, Michael. *From the 'old' to the 'new' policy design: design thinking beyond markets and collaborative governance.* Policy Sciences, v. 47, n. 3, p. 187-207, set. 2014.

HOWLETT, Michael; RAMESH, M.; PERL, Anthony. *Política Pública*: seus ciclos e subsistemas, uma abordagem integral. Rio de Janeiro: Campus/Elsevier, 2013.

LAWRENCE, Thomas B.; SUDDABY, Roy; LECA, Bernard. *Introduction: theorizing and studying institutional work.* In: ______ (Org.). Institutional work: actors and agency in institutional studies of organizations. Cambridge: Cambridge University Press, 2009. p. 1-28.

LEVITSKY, Steven; ZIBLATT, Daniel. *Como as democracias morrem.* Rio de Janeiro: Zahar, 2018.

LIN, Nan. *Social capital: a theory of social structure and action.* Cambridge: Cambridge University Press, 2001.

MARCH, James G.; SIMON, Herbert A. *Organizations.* 2 ed. Cambridge: Blackwell, 1993.

MAYNARD, S. *A evolução do sexo.* São Paulo: Unesp; 2012.

OLSON, Mancur. *A lógica da ação coletiva.* São Paulo, Edusp, 1999.

PIOVESAN, Flávia. *Direitos Humanos e o Direito Constitucional Internacional.* 15ª ed. São Paulo: Editora Saraiva, 2015.

PIOVESAN, Flávia. *Direitos humanos e justiça internacional: um estudo comparativo dos sistemas europeu, interamericano e africano.* São Paulo: Saraiva, 2013.

PUTNAM, Robert D. *Comunidade e democracia*: a experiência da Itália moderna. With Robert Leonardi and Raffaella Y

Nanetti. Rio de Janeiro: FGV, 2006.

SCHÄFER, Armin; STREECK, Wolfgang. Introduction: Poltics in The Age os Austerity. In: _______ (Org.). *Politics in The Age of Austerity*. Cambridge: Polity, 2013. p. 1-25.

SCHMIDT, Vivien A. *Discursive institutionalism: the explanatory power of ideas and discourse*. Annual Review of Political Science, v. 11, p. 303-26, jun. 2008.

SCHUMPETER, Joseph A. *The crisis of the tax state*. In: SWEDBERG, Richard (Org.). Joseph A. Schumpeter: The economics and sociology of capitalism. Princeton: Princeton University Press, 1991.

SIMON, Herbert A. (1957) *Models of Man, Social and Rational: Mathematical Essays on Rational Human Behavior in a Social Setting*. New York: John Wiley and Sons.

SIMON, Hebert A. 1990. *Invariants of human behavior*. Annu. Rev. Psychol. 41:1–19.

TAVARES, Francisco Mata Machado. *Deliberação e capitalismo*: uma crítica marxista ao pensamento de Habermas. Curitiba: Appris, 2016.

TSEBELIS, George. *Jogos ocultos*: Escolha racional no campo da política comparada. São Paulo: Edusp, 1998.